A BACKGROUND FOR GLASS
COLLECTORS

Portland Vase, late first century B.C. or early first century A.D. Height 25.4–24.8 cm. Page 28. A cased vase, mould blown and decorated on the wheel, exemplifying the acme of glass technique in antiquity. British Museum

1975 £4.00

A Background for Glass Collectors

SYLVIA COPPEN-GARDNER

PELHAM BOOKS

First published in Great Britain by PELHAM BOOKS LTD
52 Bedford Square, London WC1B 3EF
1975

ISBN 0 7207 0624 6

Set and printed in Great Britain by
Tonbridge Printers Ltd, Peach Hall Works, Tonbridge, Kent
in Baskerville eleven on thirteen point on paper supplied by
P. F. Bingham Ltd, and bound by James Burn
at Esher, Surrey

Contents

Illustrations

Acknowledgements

This book could never have been written without the encouragement, help and interest of my friends and colleagues and I am particularly indebted to Mr John Cushion.

I would like to thank Anthony Duncan, John Peet, Roland Pepper and Moira Robertson for help in preparing the manuscript, and my thanks are due to the Robert Raikes Reference Library in Gloucester and, amongst the many people who have answered my queries, to Geoffrey Frith.

Author's Note

In this guide to the appreciation and study of glass it is possible to trace the development of the glass industry from its early beginnings in antiquity to the end of the nineteenth century.

The manufacture of glass vessels is considered in relation to the historical and social background of the period, and the production and decoration of glass in a specific era is fully described in the relevant section of the book, thus avoiding needless and time-wasting cross-referencing.

Importance is given to the field of continental glass, rarely stressed in works of this kind, and there is a detailed account of both English and American glass.

It is hoped that this guide will be of value to students and to those interested in glass and intending a deeper and further study of the subject, for it is concerned with the historical study and development of a great art form, as well as taking into consideration the more practical approach of the collector.

Egyptian glass and the glass of the Ancient World

Glass almost certainly originated in Western Asia, despite the all-pervading influence of Egyptian wares in the ancient world. Glass, as an independent substance, is known to have existed from the third millennium before our era; and in Mesopotamia, one of the oldest sites of civilisation, glass was made on a very small scale as early as 2000 B.C.

Because of the crude methods of producing glass metal and the primitive and experimental state of whatever development there was, the rare objects and fragments that have survived are obviously few in number, and vessels made entirely from glass are virtually unknown until *c.* 1500 B.C. In Western Asia sites such as Tell al Rimah have revealed small pieces from glass vessels, dating from the late sixteenth century and early fifteenth century B.C., before the Egyptian glasshouses began to be effective in any way.

It is thought that Egyptian glass developed from the use of vitreous substances for glazing. The earliest Egyptian glazes of this type were applied to stone, such as steatite, which was carved and glazed in the Middle Kingdom period, *c.* 2000–1700 B.C. A thin coating of a glass-like medium was used to cover small decorative objects, such as soapstone beads or the steatite scarabs, the beetle seals of ancient Egypt, which were glazed in blue or green with something which approximated to a vitreous material. Objects such as these are very rare indeed, but glazes used at this time were identical in composition to the metal of later Egyptian glass vessels.

Egyptian glass was a light, thin, plastic soda glass made from soda, lime and sand, and was the basic metal of Mediterranean wares of the ancient world. Owing to the basic proportion of materials used in its creation, soda glass of this type required very low temperature for fusion, and glass was produced in a primitive furnace fired by wood or charcoal. It was rarely transparent at any period and was used primarily for decorative purposes.

The Egyptian word for glass was derived from that for the region of the North Western Delta where the earliest glass metal was made. In the New Kingdom in the fifteenth and fourteenth centuries B.C. glass was formed in ingots in the Delta for use in the glasshouses of Egypt. Ingots were sent to the glass-makers and were then broken up, softened and made ready for use.

Originally, Egyptian glass was made by heating the glass in a crucible and grinding it to a powder when cool. This powder was then mixed with some form of cohesive medium and spread on to a pre-made core, roughly corresponding to the shape and size of the desired article. The core and coating was then placed in a furnace and fired. This primitive and laborious method was discontinued by the time of Amenophis II, c. 1450 B.C., when the core-moulding process became the most widespread means of manufacturing glass until the discovery of glass-blowing.

Core-moulding, for which a modelled core, probably made from mud with straw as a binding, was used, allowed the shape of the glass object to be easily defined. The core, fixed to a metal rod, was wound with glass threads and subjected to heat, so as to allow for shaping and for the application of a decorative pattern by rolling on threads of a different colour. Trailed and 'combed' decoration of this kind is a feature of Egyptian work. The core was then removed and the piece ground or polished.

Because of this method of manufacture, the shapes and decoration of Egyptian glass remained almost unchanged for centuries, and it was impossible for Egyptian glass-makers to produce satisfactory large objects using their primitive techniques.

Independent glass objects, other than glass beads or the use of glass fragments in the decoration of royal ornaments, are not considered to have been made before the time of Tuthmosis III (1504–1450 B.C.) and following invasion of Western Asia it is almost certain that Asiatic glass-makers were imported into Egypt and were concerned in the manufacture of independent glass vessels. One of the earliest datable glass vessels is a small glass jug, now in the British Museum, which bears the cartouche of Tuthmosis III. There is a vessel of similar date in the Metropolitan Museum in New York.

By the time of the New Kingdom and the XVIIIth Dynasty, c. fifteenth and fourteenth centuries B.C., there was great expansion in the production of glass in Egypt, and innumerable small objects were made. However, glass of this period was essentially a highly prized luxury, and was created for a discerning and wealthy society. It was never regarded as an ordinary or everyday thing in ancient Egypt. The little Egyptian vessels, usually blue in colour, were closely derived from ceramic and hardstone prototypes.

Egyptian glass metal, made in Thebes and in other Egyptian towns, was nearly always opaque and was highly coloured. Copper and cobalt were used to make turquoise and dark blue glass. Red glass, also produced from copper, was used for surface decoration and the prevailing fashion for 'combed' patterns, trailed on the body of glass vessels, was closely related to the imitation of natural markings on semi-precious stones. Handles and feet were modelled separately and fragments of the core were often left in the roughly finished interior. The majority of such pieces, apart from glass beads, a stable export from the glasshouses of Egypt, staple exports were small containers for unguents and cosmetics. Small sculptured objects were produced by pressing molten glass into carved stone moulds. Carving was done on a very small scale by carving glass blocks on a lapidary's wheel.

15

The comparative stability of the political situation in Egypt and the strong cultural influence exerted by her upon the eastern Mediterranean helped to create a flourishing glass industry, and considerable export trade was established. Glass paste, in an elaborate design, was used to decorate the throne found in the tomb of Tutankhamun, which also contained a head rest of blue glass paste.

But it was not only in Egypt that glass was produced at this time. The Syrian glass industry was one of the largest of the ancient world and before 1200 B.C., glass was also made in Mesopotamia. The Elamite ziggurat at Choga Zanbil near Susa was decorated with glass fragments c. 1300 B.C. Glass manufactured between the Tigris and the Euphrates is rare, however, and there was probably little independent and indigenous glass-making in this area. As the Egyptian glasshouses were the foremost creators of luxury glass at this period, it was probably imported from here and from Syria.

The Syrian glass industry was profoundly influenced by Egyptian methods and by Egyptian taste. It is thought to have begun under Egyptian rule, after Tuthmosis III defeated the Canaanites in 1468 B.C., and following the invasion of Palestine and Syria. Syrian glasshouses produced very delicate glass, which was closely related in form and context to Egyptian prototypes. Glass beads and other small objects were all made by the core-moulding process. This was the only method known to glass-makers at the time and was possibly used in glasshouses in Cyprus and the Aegean was well as in Egypt, Mesopotamia and Syria.

When the Bronze Age came to an end in the eastern Mediterranean, c. 1200 B.C., there was little encouragement for the development of a well-established glass industry on a viable scale. The production of glass vessels virtually ceased with the breakdown of conditions suitable for the establishment of a settled glass trade. In Egypt, from the eleventh century B.C. there was almost total cessation in the manufacture of glass and it was not until the Saite period in the seventh and sixth centuries B.C., when Egyptian independence was re-established after Assyrian domination, that a revival in glass-making took place, and distinctive objects of good quality reappeared.

In Mesopotamia and along the Syrian coast, however, the glass industry revived from the ninth century and distinctive objects in good quality metal reappeared. A clay tablet, found in the Assurbanipal Library, c. 668–626 B.C., gives formulae for the manufacture of clear and coloured glass. The revival of manufacture in Mesopotamia and in Syria was probably a result of the widespread trade with Phoenicia, which encouraged the interchange of cultural and artistic ideas throughout the known world. Phoenician traders carried glass vessels, normally in the form of small bottles to be used as containers for Eastern cosmetics, across their trading empire and they undoubtedly had a strong influence upon the glasshouses of the day.

By the ninth century B.C. there was a small but independent glass industry in Italy. The Etruscans knew how to make glass and they set up glasshouses. Glass vessels were exported and by the fifth century, the industry had spread to the Adriatic and to Hallstatt. In the seventh or sixth centuries B.C., other small centres had started production, and glasshouses appeared in Rhodes and Cyprus, and perhaps in Greece, although the Greeks were always more concerned with the creation of fine pottery than with the production of glass vessels. There was, however, a glass furnace in the workshop of Phideas at Olympia, and glass elements were used in some of his work.

The most important producers of glass at this time were the Syrians. (Syria here represents an area along the eastern Mediterranean, between Anatolia, the ancient Cappadocia, and modern Israel, bordered on the east by the Euphrates and by the desert.) Syrian glass-makers were dependent upon what were originally Egyptian ideas and produced innumerable amphorae, the amphora being the most common form of container for liquids throughout antiquity. Syrian vessels are usually larger than those produced in Egypt and lack the sense of harmony of form and decoration which is one of the great beauties of

17

Egyptian decorative art. Like the Egyptians, the Syrians used thread ornament to decorate their wares, but on a larger and infinitely weaker scale. A feature of Syrian glass, not usually found on Egyptian work, is the use of the palm leaf as a decorative motif. Apart from amphorae and similar containers, the Syrians made small moulded dishes and amulets, and much later, in the first century A.D., Pliny wrote that glass mirrors were being made in Sidon. Some glass in this area may have been the work of Jewish craftsmen, as the Jews were concerned with glass and with glass-making from a very early date.

By the end of the fourth century, and as a result of the social and political changes caused by the widespread conquests of Alexander the Great, the glass industry of the ancient world experienced a revival, and Hellenistic influence on the shapes created by the glass-makers became apparent, so that the forms of glass after the fourth century are greatly refined and are of a more sophisticated appearance and manufacture.

Once the Achaeminian empire had ended, glass-making in Mesopotamia virtually ceased, and the Egyptian glass industry rose to prominence after the foundation of Alexandria, in 332 B.C.

In Alexandria, the leading intellectual and cultural centre of the world at this time, glass-making was revived on a large scale, and Asiatic workmen were quick to establish themselves in such a prosperous and important city. In a comparatively short time, an immense production of glass took place, and a large and influential export trade began, particularly to Greece and Italy.

Before the Alexandrian period, core-moulded glass consisted largely of vessels derived in shape from contemporary ceramics, cosmetic bottles being amongst the most common items. The small pieces of glass produced between c. 1500 B.C. and the seventh century A.D. were simple in shape and were decorated with glass threads in primitive and crude fashion. The revival of glass manufacture in the seventh century brought about a gradual and increased development in form, and decoration became far more sophisticated. The most important and highly developed pieces of glass to have survived from the ancient world and from the period prior to the establishment of the Roman Empire were made in the glasshouses of Alexandria.

There, the proliferation of glasshouses and the employment of highly skilled craftsmen, together with the existence of wealthy patrons of cultivated taste, encouraged technical experiment and the development of a greater sophistication. Alexandrian workmen, by their skill and influence, stimulated the rapid expansion of glass-making throughout the known world and Hellenistic taste gave grace and proportion to the forms in use. The techniques of making mosaic and cut glass, practised before this era, were now fully exploited and Alexandria became the glass-making centre of the world.

Mosaic glass was probably made from the fifteenth century B.C. and early fragments have been found at sites in western Asia. Mosaic vessels were made with rods of coloured glass arranged in bundles, so that the combination produced a pattern. These rods were then fused and sectioned. The patterned sections were laid on a core, corresponding with the inside of the required vessel, and loosely fixed with an adhesive. An outer mould, similar to the first, was then laid over the original core and sections, and when fused, a vessel with mosaic pattern was evolved. The surface was then ground smooth. Bowls in mosaic glass were a prominent feature of export from Alexandria. The technique was probably introduced by Asiatic workmen, as it was practised in western Asia.

Grinding and cutting were common practice in Alexandria. Grinding was used to give a smooth surface, as in the case of mosaic vessels, and to finish rough edges and irregularity. The rotating copper wheel had been developed for hardstone carving in the New Kingdom, and small vessels had been ground from glass blocks using a similar technique. This adaptation, evolved from stone cutting, was probably carried out in stone or cutting shops, rather than in the glasshouse. By the eighth century B.C. it was in widespread use.

When it was difficult to manufacture a desired form by core-moulding, a technique of pressing molten glass into an open mould was adopted. Simple moulding of this kind was commonly used in the second and first centuries for the bowls, cups and dishes which were an important export from Alexandria.

The manufacture of mosaic glass, refinements in cutting and grinding, and the exploitation of simple moulding established the continuing importance of Alexandria. Much technical experiment led to an immense improvement in glass production, but not until the discovery of blown glass did radical changes become possible.

Further reading

British Museum, *Masterpieces of Glass*, 1968.
Brooklyn, *Glass and glazes from Ancient Egypt*, 1948.
Corning, *Glass from the ancient world*, 1957.
Harden, *The glass of the Greeks and Romans*, 1935.
Honey, *Glass*, 1946.
Neuburg, *Ancient glass*, 1962.

CHAPTER TWO

Roman glass

The production of glass was one of the prime industries of the Roman Empire, and Roman glass-makers, although rarely, if ever, born in Rome, were able to establish widespread manufacture of glass vessels of all kinds and shapes, ranging in quality from superb luxury objects to ordinary commercial and household wares. Throughout the Roman world, ideas and technical development spread with remarkable speed and facility, and the constant migration of glass-makers from one part of the Empire to another encouraged the production of a range of glass vessel of extraordinary similarity. The sophisticated and stable Roman industry promoted the exploitation of far more decorative and elaborate objects than had been possible in the preceding era, and full advantage was taken of the discovery of glass-blowing.

It is not known at exactly what date blown glass first appeared, but the technique was certainly in use in the first century B.C. It was probably discovered somewhere along the Syrian coast, where some of the most important glass-making centres of antiquity were situated, and may have arisen from the practice of making moulded glass bowls. Following this development, Sidon rapidly became the most important centre for the production of objects in blown glass.

Blown glass required the use of a higher temperature than in the manufacture of moulded vessels and, by blowing the paraison, a fluid bulb of glass at the end of a metal rod, far more adventurous and individual forms could be created. The discovery of blown glass reduced the cost and labour of glass manufacture considerably, and the basic soda-glass metal, used throughout the Mediterranean world, was a perfect medium for it.

The prime importance of the glass industry within the Roman Empire lay in the development of blown glass vessels, as opposed to those simpler forms produced by the moulding process of earlier periods. Between the second century B.C. and the first century A.D., there was enormous expansion in the glass trade as a whole and the glass-making centres in Alexandria and along the Syrian coast were producing goods in large quantities. The cultivated taste of wealthy connoisseurs in the Hellenistic period and the artistic patronage of the times, together with the consolidation of Roman power, helped to create a highly favourable environment for the later expansion and consolidation of the glass industry of the Roman Empire.

During the early period of Roman development, many of the finest pieces of so-called Roman glass were probably made in Alexandria, which had been acquired by the Emperor Augustus in the Roman conquest of Egypt in 30 B.C. The Romans imported glass in vast quantities from the Alexandrian glasshouses and Egyptian and oriental workmen almost certainly worked in Italy. Throughout this period, the importance of Egypt and Syria remained predominant, as the lack of raw materials of sufficient quality made large scale production elsewhere comparatively difficult. Between the second and the fourth centuries there was a geographically wide expansion in the manufacture of glass and, with the consolidation of the Roman Empire, there was an enormous increase in the number of glasshouses. The influence of Egypt and Syria was, nevertheless, always apparent, and was an important feature in the development of Roman glass-making.

Production of glass in the Roman world was a common industrial feature. The spread of Roman colonial power and the resulting system of highly organised communications from one part of the known world to another enabled migrant glass workers to travel widely and to establish flourishing and profitable glasshouses.

Most towns in the Roman Empire possessed a glass industry of one kind or another, whilst continuous contact with the East encouraged Syrian and Alexandrian craftsmen to migrate westwards and to establish glass-making centres elsewhere.

Glass was produced in North Africa, around the Danube, in Greece, in the Greek islands, in eastern Europe, in Asia Minor and in Parthia. In western Europe, the most important centre for the manufacture of glass was in the Rhineland; glass had originally been sent there by sea, via Marseilles, and glass-makers there reflected Syrian influence. Glass vessels produced in these provincial centres were always weaker in design and in manufacture than their oriental prototypes, but there was widespread production in the majority of them, as in Cologne and the factories of the Moselle district.

Despite the exploitation of blown glass and the consequent increase in production, Roman glass was essentially handwork, using comparatively primitive tools and with furnaces fired by wood or charcoal. In the Roman period, the use and manufacture of simple glass vessels spread throughout the known world, and pieces in this category were small, plain, simple monochrome vessels of thin, blue, green or green soda glass, with little decoration.

The colour of Roman glass varies, according to the amount of iron present in the glass sands. Roman glass normally contained $71\frac{1}{2}$ per cent silica and approximately $16\frac{1}{2}$ per cent soda. It was not until the second century A.D., or possibly slightly earlier, that Roman glass-makers were able to neutralise the green tints apparent in contemporary metal and were able to manufacture colourless glass by the addition of manganese. Clear and transparent glass was greatly prized in the Roman world, and blue glass, obtained with the use of copper or cobalt, and red glass, obtained from copper, were comparatively rare.

The iridescence of Roman glass, which appears to be a common feature of this period, is entirely unintentional on the part of the original glass-maker and is a form of metal-sickness, caused by exposing the glass to damp earth or humidity. Carbon dioxide dissolving in a moist atmosphere forms carbonic acid and this process, in conjunction with alkali in the glass metal, creates decomposition. A film appears on the surface of the object, giving the effect of a metallic lustre, and glass which has been de-colourised by the use of manganese is more prone to iridescence than is coloured metal. The chemical decomposition also reduces the overall weight of the object, so that glass of this type appears to be, and often is, extremely light.

Roman glass is usually decorated in three ways : by tooling, by the application of glass threads or by engraving.

Tooled decoration, obtained by manipulating, pinching and indenting the warm glass with metal tools, is one of the basic and most common forms of Roman ornament and was used primarily in the decoration of the more mundane and everyday vessels. It was commonly used in the decoration of the applied handles which appear on the small glass containers of the Roman world.

In the decoration of such objects, tooling and the application of warm, drawn threads of glass on to a warm vessel were occasionally carried out upon the same piece, the applied threads being used to create a decorative surface on objects of relatively simple form. A lump of glass was attached to the glass body, usually a vase. The vase was then spun while the glass thread was drawn out. Decoration of this type was sometimes carried out in relief and sometimes marvered to the main body. Blobs or drops of glass metal were also used to provide surface decoration. They were applied and then fused by heating.

The technique of cutting and engraving glass, which had been known to the Egyptians, was greatly exploited by the Romans. Cold glass was incised with a graving tool and the rough parts of the design were then smoothed and polished into facets, with the help of a rotating wheel fed with water and corundum. In elaborate forms of decoration, a graving tool was used again to heighten and embellish the design. The more skilled designs of the later Roman period were virtually lapidaries' work and here only a graving tool was used. Embellishment of this kind was largely used to create mythological decoration, although Christian symbolism appears in fourth-century work. Engraving, unlike tooling or application, was almost invariably used alone.

The development of the Roman glass industry consists of three more or less distinctive periods of stylistic and technical achievement; namely, the Early Imperial period of the first century A.D., the Middle Imperial period of the second and third centuries, and the Later Imperial period of the fourth and fifth centuries. These particular groupings enable one to give an approximation as to the dating of Roman glass vessels, although one should bear in mind that the more ordinary pieces of glass produced throughout the Roman world changed very little and are remarkably similar in appearance from one part of the Empire to another.

In the Early Imperial period of the first century, glass technology and an interest in its production was mentioned by several of the classical writers. After the Egyptian conquest of Augustus in 30 B.C., glass became a fashionable and expensive luxury for the wealthy and sophisticated home market, despite the immense cost of importing glass vessels from Egypt and Syria. As the export trade from Egypt grew, so the imported goods became less costly and, c. A.D. 14, Alexandrian craftsmen founded glasshouses between Cumae and Liturnum, at Puteoli, and at the Porta Caserna in Rome. These early Roman glasshouses, using Volturnus sand, undoubtedly employed workmen from Egypt and Syria. It was from such small centres that glass-working, encouraged by migrant craftsmen, spread out from Rome across the Roman Empire.

The geographer, Strabo, an Alexandrian Greek who was born in 63 B.C. and educated in Rome, and lived in Alexandria

between 25 and 20 B.C., took an informed interest in the manufacture of glass and in the glass industry of the day. Strabo is
thought to have visited the famous Alexandrian glasshouses and
in 7 B.C., he visited the glass-works on the Syrian coast. In
his writings, he mentions that glass-makers were experimenting
in the improvement of coloured glass and that experiments were
being made in easier methods of production. He also noted the
manufacture of crystal-clear glass. It is possible that, at this
period, the Syrians were becoming conscious of Egyptian competition in the rising and profitable Roman market. Glass-
makers everywhere were enlarging their output and expanding
production and the development of new techniques, in order to
comply with the huge demand for glass at this time.

There is considerable mention of glass in Pliny's *Natural
History*. Pliny, who was born in A.D. 23, considered Tyre and
Sidon as the most important glass-making centres in the world,
and described the latter as *'Sidon artifex vitri'* (Sidon, the town
of the glass craftsmen). Throughout the first century, work
produced in the oriental factories was of greater skill and of
higher quality than that of the western Empire, despite the
presence of oriental craftsmen in the west and the use of forms
derived from oriental prototypes.

The Early Imperial period was distinguished by the rapid
expansion of glass manufacture throughout the Empire and by
the increasing skill of glass-makers in provincial centres. As
technical skill improved and as decorative technique evolved,
so glasshouses were set up across the Roman world and by the
middle of the first century, they had been established in Gaul,
where glass-makers from the eastern Mediterranean had
migrated to Boulogne, to Amiens, to Namur and to Rheims, as
well as to Germany and the Alpine provinces. These provincial
concerns were never as sophisticated in production as those of
the eastern Empire, although glass-making centres such as
Cologne were of some importance.

Roman glass of the first century is decorative, often elaborate
and, in the hands of Egyptian or of Syrian craftsmen, of a very

high standard. Coloured and polychrome glass and pillar moulded bowls, with decoration like that of the gadrooning on silver, were very popular. Pliny mentions that glass was used as a feature of interior decoration and describes a glass sculpture, reproducing the features of the Emperor Augustus, in opaque red metal. Painted enamel work, derived from Alexandrian decoration, was produced, and some fired enamelling has been ascribed to the Rhineland factories. Elaboration and exotic colouring were greatly admired in this period. Glass vessels of a more exotic and sophisticated variety were usually the work of oriental craftsmen and were decorative rather than strictly practical.

Pliny, writing in A.D. 77, mentions the general improvement in manufacture, and factory production was a common feature of the Roman glass industry. Factories, owned by Greeks or by Hellenised orientals, produced marked goods, and mould-blown vessels bearing signatures in Greek characters appear in the Early Imperial period. *Nicon, Triphon, Jason,* who is known to have had a workshop in Rome, and *Ennion,* the most famous signature on marked and mould-blown vessels, date from this time. *Ennion,* like *Jason,* produced work in Italy. Fourteen known pieces, all cups, survive from his factory, eleven of which were found in northern Italy.

The influence of contemporary pottery upon glass forms such as these was apparent as Roman glass developed. In the reign of Tiberius (A.D. 14–37) pottery, particularly Samian ware, was highly regarded in the European market and had a marked effect upon glass design. The shapes of mould-blown vessels, decorated in relief, which had considerable vogue in the Early Imperial period, were adapted from contemporary pottery. The small, moulded drinking cups with moulded relief decoration, derived from cut-glass, depicting scenes from the popular Roman circus, are examples of this type and were of widespread popularity. Silver vessels were also of importance in the creation of new form. Bronze, silver and gold plate was used in wealthy Roman households and had a similar effect upon glassware created for the same purpose, which had to be adapted to assume the function of plate.

The most important pieces of glass of the Early Imperial period were those produced by oriental craftsmen, and elaborate cut-glass was greatly prized. Lathe cutting, probably developed in the Alexandrian workshops in the first century B.C., was fully utilised to superb effect; cameo cutting was a feature of such work. An opaque blown vessel, usually of a coloured metal, was cased with another colour glass and marvered. The outer layer of opaque white metal was then cut away using the lapidaries' technique; shadow in the design was produced by variation in the thickness of the cutting. These cameo glasses would have been the property of wealthy connoisseurs and were great works of art in their own right. The most famous is the Portland Vase, now in the British Museum, where was made in the late first century B.C. or in the first century A.D., almost certainly by oriental craftsmen. It was copied by Josiah Wedgwood (1786–1790) and re-created in glass in the nineteenth century by John Northwood (1873–1876).

Glass cutting, as such, probably developed from the practice of polishing *murrhine* bowls, mentioned by Pliny in the Early Imperial period. These glass vessels were possibly rotary polished on the inside. Egyptian *murrhines* were fashionable in Italy before this time. *Murrhine* bowls are thought to have been polychrome mosaic or *millefiori* vessels, originally of patterned semi-precious stones, and copied by glass-makers to achieve the same effect. Coloured glass was highly desirable in the Roman luxury trade and by the time of Nero (A.D. 54–68) it was fashionable to collect glass objects of all kinds, most of which must have been imported in order to meet the more sophisticated demand.

Despite the fashion for coloured and decorative glass that was prevalent throughout the first century, there was an interest in clear and colourless glass, although a totally clear glass metal, refined with the addition of manganese, was not in current use until the second century. The imitation of semi-precious and strangely marked stones was eventually replaced with the use of clear glass and vessels cut from a block and emulating rock-crystal became of greater importance. Pliny, in his *Natural History*, mentions the popularity and desirability of transparent glass resembling rock-crystal and states that it had displaced the use of gold and silver. Rock-crystal itself, despite the interest aroused by imitative glassware, was one of the status symbols of the age and was enormously expensive.

Glass produced in the first century was often fragile, and in the fifties Seneca (*c.* 4 B.C.–A.D. 65) complained that its price had become inflated because of this fragility.

It was not, however, until the Middle Imperial period of the second and third centuries that Roman manufacture achieved its full potential, with blown glass being produced in large quantities throughout the Empire. During this period, the Gallic glasshouses and the glass-making centres of Cologne and Trier were at their height. There was widespread use of glass for burial purposes, either in the form of cinerary urns or household goods placed in the grave.

Glass-blowing was fully exploited throughout the Roman Empire at this time and was in widespread use in the production of comparatively cheap goods. The migration of oriental workmen who encouraged the use of similar methods and designs throughout the known world meant that the provincial glasshouses in the western Empire were ultimately producing blown goods of a standard comparable with that of more sophisticated centres elsewhere.

Aquileia, near Trieste, the ninth city of the Roman world and a highly important manufacturing and commercial town, was a centre for glass-cutting and, by the third century, controlled a very large proportion of this trade. There is a recorded dispute of this period between the glass manufacturers and the cutters; the latter were by this time divided into a separate trade, so that cutting was carried out in decorating workshops rather than in the actual glasshouses.

Despite the popularity and large production of cut-glass, glass

metal was still fragile – the fault of materials used in its creation. As the glass cooled and contracted, tensions appeared on
the surface. Such tensions were disturbed in the cutting and the
vessels were liable to crack. In the dispute in Aquileia, the
manufacturers accused the cutters of damaging and thus spoiling
the blanks sent from the glasshouses to be decorated.

Another important feature of the Middle Imperial period was
the use of gold glass. This process was known in the Hellenistic
period of the third century B.C., examples of which are the
vessels found at Canosa. Gold glass of the Roman era, however,
is usually associated with Christian symbolism, although it is
not necessarily Christian and there are many pieces with pagan
decoration. It was in use in the third and fourth centuries. The
vessel itself was rarely coloured and was made from transparent
layers, enclosing engraved decoration in gold leaf. Glass vessels
such as these were almost certainly made in Rome or somewhere near it. Examples, with the glass bowl broken away to
leave only the decorated base, were found embedded in the
walls in the Catacombs.

In this period, colourless glass virtually replaced the coloured
and elaborate vessels of the first century. One of the most
common decorative features was the extensive use of snake-
thread ornament, whereby vessels were decorated in serpentine
fashion with trailed threads of applied glass of varying thickness.
Eastern glass-makers produced more sophisticated ornaments of
this kind, but the fashion was used constantly throughout the
Empire.

Mould-blown head flasks were popular in the second and
third centuries, as were *Frontinus flasks,* which were made in
Gaul, either in Boulogne or in Amiens, in the third and fourth
centuries. The *Frontinus flasks,* named after the factory in
which they were made, were moulded, keg-shaped flasks, with
hoop-like rings at top and bottom, possibly derived in form
from barrels, and were a feature of glass manufacture of the
western Empire.

So important was the glass industry that the Emperor Constantine, who died in A.D. 337, raised the status of glass-makers to that of goldsmiths and artists. The glass-makers were segregated into two independent and totally separate bodies, the *vitriarii,* the blowers and decorators of glass, and the *diatretarii,* those who cut and engraved it.

The desire for cut and decorated glass is exemplified in the Later Imperial period by elaborately worked *diatreta* or cagecups, an example of which is the fourth century Lycurgus Cup, now in the British Museum. It has been said that the openwork casing on such pieces was inspired by vessels blown into silver mounts and the design of the cups, covered with a fine and decorative exterior network of glass, certainly suggests an influence of this kind. The techniques used for the *diatreta,* which represent the finest examples of Roman glass-cutting, were derived from the cutting and drilling used upon semi-precious stones and cameo glass. To produce works of art such as these involved superb skill, as the metal, like that of all Roman glass, was extremely fragile and the cutting was virtually lapidaries' work.

Cage-cups display considerable diversity in ornament. They are thought to have been made by dipping a transparent glass vessel into molten coloured glass or by enclosing it in a coloured glass bubble. Slips of yet another colour, if desired, were then wound round the cased glass and marvered in. After heating to ensure complete fusion, the vessel was ground on a lathe and the decoration carried out on the wheel. In the case of a one-colour vessel there was probably no surface application, the 'cage' being produced by undercutting. Such a practice is indicated by the flow of the air bubbles in both form and ornament.

Apart from luxury objects, such as the Lycurgus cup, which were produced for a wealthy and sophisticated society and were exceptional works of art in their own right, utilising cutting in one form or another, the glasshouses of the Roman Empire produced an endless series of containers for commercial and household use. Containers of every conceivable kind were made, from small toilet vessels to massive ones for commercial and storage purposes. Glass containers such as these were of great value in the widespread trade of the Roman world, as they were lighter and more durable for transport than comparable pottery vessels. They were used extensively throughout the Roman Empire, and were strengthened for transportation by the addition of plaited covers.

The largest production was in the manufacture of glass vessels for domestic use and this was of course greatly facilitated by the extensive practice of glass-blowing. Rapid expansion of trade and good communications throughout the Roman world enabled the glass-makers to make a significant contribution to the economy, and ordinary household wares were produced in large quantities.

Roman glass vessels appear as a common feature in tombs of the period, particularly following the widespread practice of cremation in the Western Empire in the second century. The ashes of the cremated were sometimes placed in glass containers, and small glass objects appear as tomb furniture far more frequently than similar objects in pottery. Glass vessels of the household variety found in Roman tombs were not necessarily of everyday origin, but they do represent common and contemporary forms of domestic glassware.

Flat glass dishes are comparatively rare in the range of household goods made in the Roman world. Bowls, cups, flasks and jugs are the most widespread form to have survived, and in the Karanis hoard found in Egypt, dating from the second and fifth centuries A.D., which contained a large number of cheap, blown wares for domestic and table use, lamp glasses were also found. Lamp glasses were small vessels made to be set in stands or hung in groups, and were a common feature in Roman households. They contained a wick in a metal holder or on a float, and were filled with water on which oil had been poured.

All later European glass was profoundly influenced by the world-wide domination of the Roman glass trade. The Roman glass industry effectively laid the foundations on which European development began, and pioneered techniques in production and methods of manufacture which were never entirely forgotten after the collapse of the Roman Empire.

Further reading

British Museum, *Masterpieces of Glass,* 1968.
Harden, *The Glass of the Greeks and Romans,* 1935.
Honey, *Glass,* 1946.
Thorpe, *The Prelude to European Cut Glass,* 1938.

CHAPTER THREE

Early European and Islamic glass

Towards the end of the late Imperial period, the power of
Roman rule within the Empire was menaced, not only by
internal dissension but by invasion from migratory and bar-
barian hordes, and glass-making in Europe began to decline.
Political and social upheaval, the collapse of law and order and
the consequent breakdown in communications did not provide
a suitable or satisfactory environment for the production of
glass.

The manufacture of glass on such a widespread scale in the
preceding era suffered a setback for a variety of reasons. Frankish invasions in contemporary Belgium in A.D. 256 and 276
and the establishment of the seat of government by Constantine
in Constantinople, the rebuilt Byzantium of A.D. 324, together
with subsequent cultural development in the east rather than
in the west of the Empire, all meant that the art of the west,
without the stimulus provided from the east and without the
encouragement of the political and social ties which had so
profoundly influenced the earlier period, began to decline, and
the production of glass was very soon to reflect the important
and influential changes apparent in the cultural pattern of the
age.

The decline of the Western Empire by the fifth century,
ever-increasing danger from invasion and the total destruction
of satisfactory and suitable conditions for the continuing practice

of glass-making were important factors in reducing the former strength of the industry in western Europe. Glass vessels made in this area, following the early years of the century, are indicative of such an upheaval. From this time onwards, glass-making suffered from serious deterioration in technique and in the use of form and decoration. Glass vessels produced in the so-called Dark Ages bear little relation, either in quality or in form, with those made during the Roman period.

The output of the Western Empire had rarely achieved the sophistication apparent in glass-making centres of the east, and the taste for alcohol in northern Europe encouraged the glass-makers of the Western Empire to manufacture a higher proportion of drinking vessels than would have been required elsewhere. Cosmetic and unguent bottles were never the most important aspect of production in western glasshouses, where the crudity of northern influence was always latent in the forms and decoration of glass vessels.

The successful glass industry in the far Western Empire diminished with the destruction of Roman rule by the Frankish invasions in A.D. 406. In the Frankish-Merovingian period, from the fifth to the ninth centuries what glass there was tended to be a weak and crude version of Roman provincial output. Glass continued to be made, on a very small scale in comparison with Roman production, but the vessels created were of decidedly inferior quality and reflected the crudity of taste in an age of barbarism and of almost total decadence.

The discontinuation of the burial of grave goods, a practice forbidden by the Church, and the disuse of glass vessels for ritual purposes as established in the Merovingian period, resulted in the survival of few vessels from these frequently troubled and unsettled times. The manufacture of glass vessels in any quantity whatsoever gradually came to an end and glass of this period is exceedingly rare. From this time onwards the production of glass in western Europe virtually ceased. In the so-called Dark Ages, even if technical expertise could have been maintained against such an unpromising and uncompromising background, there would have been little or no demand for the sophistication apparent in Roman glass.

Glass metal used at this time was essentially that of the Roman world. In many areas, the problem of obtaining suitable raw materials for use in the manufacture of glass must have been an almost insuperable one, due to the destruction of established trade routes and to the general instability of contemporary society. It has been stated that in the unsettled period following the first Frankish invasions of the third century, Belgian glass-makers were obliged to abandon the use of the soda ash formerly acquired through trade with the Mediterranean coast. In order to replace this essential constituent in the manufacture of the common glass metal of the period, it is thought that some glass-makers made use of plant ash, obtained from bracken and similar forest plants, although the use of *waldglas,* made with plant ash, did not become widespread until the end of the eleventh century.

The glass at this time was not only imperfect and of poor clarity, due to general impurity of the metal, but was equally poor in colour. The vessels themselves were frequently flawed, with visible bubbles and striations. The metal was generally greenish in tone, often darker in appearance than similar Roman glass, and with a pronounced brown or yellow tinge. The presence of iron oxide, always a factor to be considered in glass manufacture, was not correctly dispelled, as had been the practice in the Roman world, causing sometimes strangely effective and rare colouring, probably due to scientific maladjustment rather than to the intention of the craftsmen. Colour such as blue is rarely found before the seventh century in glass vessels of this type.

Glass of this period is invariably blown, but the highly developed technique used by glass-makers of the Roman Empire was soon abandoned. Mould blowing was in use on a very simple scale and Teutonic glass was usually of comparatively plain form, with very little decoration.

Such relatively unsophisticated objects, however, were frequently adorned with skilled trailed ornament, either in the form of threads, applied in spiral form, as in some of the claw beakers and simple vessels of the period, or in thickened and more exaggerated fashion, as in the decoration applied to vessels, such as drinking horns.

Drinking vessels, for which there was a great demand in the Dark Ages, normally had no foot, so that the simple horn and beaker shapes had to be drained before they were set down. This peculiar feature may not have been solely dictated by the customary habits of the time, but possibly resulted from the general decadence in glass-making technique. Rims of this period are of a rough and unfinished appearance. The long, conical or bag-shaped cups, the drinking horns and claw beakers reflect the crudity of everyday life, and the claw beakers are the most memorable of the three.

The use of the *prunt* or applied drop of glass, known to Roman craftsmen, was rarely practised in the ancient world, but was exploited greatly and to superb effect in the Dark Ages. Such decoration is closely related to that created by the use of thread ornament, but *prunts* were dropped on the surface, rather than trailed on. Ornament of this kind was applied to beakers of roughly cylindrical appearance and with a rounded base or, rarely, with a very small foot. Such vessels probably derived from a late Roman glass form, thought to have been made in Cologne, on which there was prototype surface application of this kind. Early claw beakers were decorated with applied drops or spots of glass which closely resemble hooks. Later on, such characteristic ornament was hollow and was applied in the form of a claw, or as a surface projection with the appearance of an elephant's trunk, hence the German name of *Rüsselbecher*. These projections were blown hollow from within the vessel. A heated drop of glass was applied on the outside of the object, thus effectively warming the surface. The drop was then blown hollow and manipulated with tongs, so as to achieve the characteristic claw. The use of ornament such as this was at its height by the late fifth or early sixth centuries, and was still practised in the early part of the eighth century.

It is virtually impossible to give an accurate attribution as to place of origin for this type of vessel. The glass that has survived from the Dark Ages has been found almost invariably on the site of pagan burial, and it is conceivable that grave goods of this kind would have been brought from further afield, as is almost certainly the case with pieces of glass found in England. The migratory pattern of contemporary society gave rise to a similarity in style in northern and western Europe, but it is unrealistic to ascribe a definitive place of origin to vessels produced in such a confused and turbulent age.

In England, following the departure of the Romans and during the almost total chaos which ensued, glass-making could hardly have survived, even on a very small scale, and the manufacture of glass vessels must soon have come to an end. In the seventh and eighth centuries, the monks at Wearmouth are recorded as having asked for glass-makers to come from Gaul and the Rhineland, thus emphasising the complete breakdown in glass production which must have been of common occurrence in many parts of Europe.

In the East, however, the situation with regard to the manufacture of glass was totally different. Between the fall of the Roman Empire and the establishment of Islam rule in the seventh century, the glass-making centres of the Roman world remained in almost full operation, post-classical vessels being made in a decadent version of Roman form. The ascendance of Islam and the establishment of overall Arab domination did not seriously affect the flourishing and long-established glass trade, or have any immediate influence upon the forms in use.

From A.D. 661 to 750, the Umayyad Dynasty rule Islam from Syria, but in 750 the centre of the ARAB Empire moved to Baghdad on the accession of the Abbasid rulers, thus establishing a total and distinctive Islamic culture. The united Arab world, ruled by one ruler and extending from western Asia to the southern Mediterranean, soon achieved political and artistic importance, and it is from this period that unique forms of decorative ornament appear in the manufacture of Islamic glass.

This period of social stabiolity and great cultural impetus demanded the creation of sophisticated and elegant glass vessels, and glass-makers were encouraged to produce highly decorative and technically elaborate work.

During excavations conducted between 1912 and 1914 by German archaeologists at Samarra, the centre of Abbasid culture from 836 to 883, glass made in this early Islamic period was discovered, some of which was probably the work of Egyptian craftsmen rather than of native glass-makers. Migrant craftsmen undoubtedly travelled to such centres as Baghdad to attract Court patronage and to profit by it. Mosaic work, akin to Alexandrian *Millefiore,* was found at Samarra, together with a number of small perfume bottles and a quantity of fragmented cut-glass.

The manufacture of glass cut with the wheel was well established in Islamic production by the ninth century, particularly in Baghdad and Basra. Persian influence, so apparent in early Islamic decorative art, may have given rise to this development. Cut-glass, a form of decoration practised during the rule of the Sassanian Emperors (224–651), was again produced under the Samarrid Dynasty (819–1004).

The cut-glass of the early Islamic period was comparatively simple in design, with an emphasis upon the use of cut facets and with some abstract forms cut as part of the decoration. Bevelling, where the outline of the ornament was cut on a slant, was a feature observed in the decorative carving and stucco found at Samarra. This technique was later used in Persia, Egypt and Northern Africa for the decoration of glass, as well as in wood and plaster work.

Islamic glass-cutters also elaborated upon an infinitely more sophisticated possibility. From the ninth century, vessels were decorated with relief ornament of considerable complexity in which the surface was ground away with the same technique as that used by the cutters of rock crystal. This form of decoration was certainly influenced by lapidaries' work.

From the tenth to the thirteenth centuries, cutting was of paramount importance. Cameo cutting, as practised in the ancient world, is very rarely in evidence and there are few pieces dating from this early period. Diamond point engraving was seldom practised, but the methods of moulding and pincered work of the Roman era continued, as did the combed decoration and thread ornament found in Egyptian glass of antiquity.

Islamic glass-makers also decorated vessels with lustre painting, similar to that first used in Mesopotamia, from the ninth century, in the decoration of tin-glazed earthenware. Glass vessels with lustrous ornament of extreme delicacy, imperceptible to the touch, were possibly produced in Egypt and perhaps later in Syria. Some of the decoration may be of an earlier date than that of the lustre painting applied to ceramics. The technique, however, is not yet fully identified and decoration of this kind, either in the use of coloured pigments or in the use of pigments intended to represent a metallic lustre, is extremely rare.

It is uncommon to find true enamel painting, or gilding, before the end of the Fatimid Dynasty in 1171. In the late twelfth century, a new style of pottery was developed in Raqqa in Syria and it is thought that concurrent with this development, Egyptian glass-makers migrated to Syria and to northwestern Mesopotamia. Glass decorated with fired, coloured enamels was produced at this time and Egyptian gilding was introduced as a means of further adornment. Decorative glass vessels of this type were never made elsewhere, with the exception of the 'Fustat' glass made in Egypt, c. 1270–1340.

Islamic enamelled glass of the thirteenth and fourteenth centuries was one of the greatest art forms of the period, but in many cases it is difficult to give a definite place of origin. Migrant glass-makers, attracted by the patronage extended by various princely rulers, tended to travel far, so there are few purely local styles and the use of decorative motifs depended upon the individual glass-maker, rather than on the place from which he originated or in which he was working.

Enamelled glass is thought to have been made in Raqqa between *c.* 1170 and 1270, in Aleppo from *c.* 1250, prior to the Mongol destruction of 1260, and in Damascus from *c.* 1250 to 1300. Syrian work of this kind was justifiably renowned and glass vessels were occasionally introduced into Europe, particularly during the period of the Crusades. Tyre and Aleppo were notable centres of glass-making and until the Sultan Khadil seized Acre in 1291 and expelled the Franks from Syria, some Syro-Frankish glass was made; the few remaining pieces supposedly come from one decorating workshop, that of Magister Aldrovandini, who was probably an Italian working as a decorator in Syria and whose workshop was producing glass from about 1260 to 1290 somewhere in Latin territory. It is conceivable, however, that the name Magister Aldrovandini, which appears on a glass now in the British Museum, does not refer to a specific workman or to a workshop, but rather to the commissioner of the vessel. The origin of supposedly Syro-Frankish pieces is in some doubt and it is possible that vessels of this kind may have originated either in Venice or in the Rhineland rather than in Syria.

The simple enamelled drinking vessels of the late twelfth and early thirteenth centuries were of transparent and clear metal, frequently imperfect and inclined to be rather thick. When the glass vessel was cold, an ornament in heavy, opaque vitreous enamel was outlined in red and then fired.

The thirteenth century saw the beginning of the greatest period in the production of enamelled glass. The glass metal was seldom colourless, being of a greenish brown. Sophisticated ornament in fusible enamel was occasionally used in the decoration of coloured glass, blue metal being created with the use of cobalt, and purple with the use of manganese. Such enamelling is of two very distinctive types.

The first type, decorative enamel work in rich colours, with elaborate and often complex ornament and with figurative decoration, is ascribed either to Aleppo or to Kadesia on the Tigris, near Samarra, which was famous for glass-making at this time. This ornamental enamelling may also be the product of decorating workshops in Baghdad, which fell to the Mongols in 1258, or could have been made in Mossul in Mesopotamia. Following the Mongol invasion of Iraq, however, such work must have been carried out in Syria and the finest Islamic enamelling upon glass is undoubtedly of Syrian origin. The decoration, created with the use of brilliant blue and red enamels, together with opaque white and with heavily applied gilding, was occasionally applied to the back of the vessel. Decorative enamelling of this first type is closely related to that of Persian ceramics and is akin to the inlaid bronze from Mossul and to the gold and silver inlay produced in Syria at this time. The figurative decoration is derived from Persian miniature painting and from painting of the Baghdad school.

The second type of enamelled ornament is thought to have been produced in Damascus, an important glass-making centre. Here, the fired enamelling is sparingly used and fine delineation of ornament and of decorative borders is a feature.

The destruction of Baghdad in 1258, and Mongol raids on Damascus in 1260 and again in 1300, together with the founding of the Mongol Dynasty in China in 1280, gave rise to the use of distinctly Chinese ornament. Chinese influence, apparent on contemporary ceramics, was in evidence throughout the fourteenth century when glass was exported from Syria in exchange for oriental porcelain. The use of motifs inspired by Chinese art resulted in glass vessels with naturalistic ornament of Chinese derivation, such as paeonies, the phoenix, vines and lotus flowers.

From the early thirteenth century, the blue enamel used by Islamic glass-makers was of a totally different colour from before, more like lapis lazuli. This heavier colouring appears upon the series of mosque lamps in production at the end of the thirteenth century and throughout the fourteenth.

Mosque lamps are possibly the most famous of all pieces of Islamic glass. They were rarely of coloured metal and, as they were produced for mosques and religious institutions, they did not bear any representation to human form, the use of which had been forbidden by the Prophet. Enamelled ornament on mosque lamps showed dedicatory inscriptions and quotations from the Koran, and the work is unsigned, with the exception of the work of Alī Bin Muhammad Amāki (or al Ramaki, or al Zamaki), c. 1330.

The lamps were adorned with armorial ornament as well as with dedicatory and religious texts. They were a feature of the decorative art of the period of the Mameluke rulers in Egypt, and armorial decoration of this kind is representative of a blazon awarded by the Sultan and refers to a particular office. Although the decoration is associated with Egypt, the lamps themselves were of Syrian origin.

Mosque lamps were not lamps in the true sense, but lanterns or shades. They were made to surround an inner vessel in which oil was burned. A series of chains was passed through a glass ball and attached to rings, so that the vessel could be suspended from the roof. Early mosque lamps usually had three rings, whilst the later vessels of the fourteenth century had six. The lamps themselves are symbolic of the words of the Prophet, often included as part of their decoration : 'God is the light of the heavens and the earth; His light is as a niche in which is a lamp; the lamp in a glass; the glass as it were a glittering star.'

The decoration, particularly the calligraphic inscription, was of superb quality and is very like the calligraphic ornament upon 'Damascened' metal; brass embellished with gold and silver. The enamelling on early mosque lamps was derived from that practised on secular pieces of the so-called Damascus type and was used on lamps of the early three-ringed variety. Chinese motifs and strap-work were incorporated in the decoration at a later period, but the general standard of the enamelled ornament of the late fourteenth century is very inferior compared with that of the first part of the century. The later decoration reflects the general decline in the enamelling of this period, when mosque lamps made up the largest proportion of the output from Islamic glasshouses.

The destruction of Damascus by Timur in 1400, and the invasion of Aleppo and of northern Syria brought the Islamic glass industry to an end. Timur removed skilled craftsmen such as the glass-makers from Damascus to Samarqand, and the manufacture of glass in Syria virtually ceased. The production of the Islamic glasshouses in the Near East never regained its former importance and in the fifteenth century, the Venetians are recorded as having sent mosque lamps from Murano to Damascus, thus establishing the low level to which Syrian output had declined.

'Hedwig' glasses

Amongst the pieces of decorative glass ascribed to Islamic production, there exist several beakers of uncertain provenance, described as 'Hedwig' glasses. This series is named afer a particular example once supposedly in the possession of St Hedwig, the Patron Saint of Silesia, who died in 1243. They were possibly brought into Europe during the period of the Crusades and being regarded as suitable vessels for the enshrinement of holy relics, were placed in Cathedral Treasuries.

'Hedwig' glasses are beaker-shaped, made in a heavy and colourless metal, and are between 10.2 cm and 15.2 cm in height. The unique quality of pronounced individual form which is characteristic of such vessels lies in the deep and linear cameo cutting with which they are decorated. This cutting and the use of motifs such as lions, griffins and eagles, is closely related to that used to decorate rock crystal and, in consequence, they have been ascribed to eleventh- or twelfth-century Egypt. There is, however, some doubt about their exact origins. They have been further ascribed as being the product of Egyptian cutting in a western workshop, or as belonging to the Kingdom of Kiev.

Further reading

Chambon, *L'histoire de la Verrerie en Belgique du lle siècle à nos jours,* 1955

Honey, *Burlington Magazine* 'Syrian glass', 1927.

Honey, *Glass,* 1946.

Mayer, *Islamic glass workers and their work,* 1954.

CHAPTER FOUR

Venetian glass

The Venetian glass trade was already a well-established and commercial proposition by the beginning of the fifteenth century. The combination of the destruction of the industry in the Near East and the added stimulus given to the artistic development of the century through the inspiration of the Renaissance, enabled Venetian glass-makers to establish complete domination of the European glass trade throughout the fifteenth century, so creating a pattern for the development of glass-making in the following period, when glasshouses on the Venetian model were set up throughout Europe.

The geographical and political situation of Venice enabled the creation of a widespread trading empire from a comparatively early period in European history, and by the twelfth century the Venetians were in full control of the Adriatic and the route to the Holy Land. The fall of Byzantium in 1204 extended their power in the Near East, with the later protection of trade routes and the development of Venetian colonisation encouraging the expansion of Venetian trade throughout the Islamic world. The foundation for the enormous and unchallenged maritime and commercial importance of fifteenth-century Venice was thus established.

The Venetians constantly sought trading supremacy and, in particular, monopoly in the glass industry. The production of glass, increasing in importance and in output throughout the

Renaissance, was one of the few industries native to Venice in which it was possible to establish immense commercial profit on a wide scale. The glass industry was therefore regarded as being one of vital importance to the economy.

This aspect and the political stability of the Venetian Empire encouraged the establishment of a highly developed industry. State protection enabled the glass-makers to experiment in methods of manufacture and in the production of elaborate and fantastic glass vessels exemplifying the splendour of the Renaissance. Glass-makers were given every encouragement to develop their trade and to expand their output.

The manufacture of glass was not, however, a new feature. It had been encouraged in Venice for some considerable time before the fall of Damascus in 1400, and had been established long before the fifteenth century.

The development of glass in and around Venice followed the tradition and technique established in the Roman period, when a considerable amount of glass was made along the Adriatic coast, and it was from this long-established Roman tradition that the Venetian industry was ultimately derived.

After the collapse of the Roman Empire and the subsequent decline in the production of glass vessels, it is possible that the tradition of mosaic work and the stimulus given to the decorative arts by monastic influence enabled continuing production of glass on a very small scale, thus establishing the basis from which the later industry developed. The long tradition in glass-making and close commercial ties between Venice and the Near East must have encouraged the rise of the industry, and by the end of the tenth century, there were probably glass-makers in Venice itself – possibly native glass-makers rather than oriental workmen making glass on the Islamic pattern. Very little is known about the vessels produced at this time, but the glass metal must have been of simple manufacture and the vessels themselves would have been of relatively crude and simple form. Any glass of a more sophisticated type would almost certainly have been imported into Venice from the Near

East. It is also possible that craftsmen came into Venice from Byzantium and Syria.

By the eleventh century, the industry was well established and Venetian glass-makers are recorded as having been in contact with Alexandria, which, although no longer one of the greatest centres for the production of glass as it had been in the ancient and Roman world, was still of importance. Commercial links between the Near East and Venice were always close and the development of the Venetian decorative arts reflected this influence, which was exploited by the Venetians to full extent.

By 1291, Venetian glasshouses were established on the lagoon outside Venice. By placing the glasshouses on the island of Murano, the Venetian authorities not only protected the city of Venice from fire, a hazard of early glass-making, but also ensured State protection and government regulation of trade. The glass industry thus became a monopoly of the State under rigidly enforced control. Workmen on Murano virtually became prisoners of the Republic, and were condemned to death for treachery if they left Venice to practise their craft elsewhere. This system was designed to further the establishment of a European monopoly. In return for such authoritarian rule over the glass trade, the island was granted the right to a more democratic system of government than that of Venice itself.

The manufacture of some small objects was continued in the city of Venice, despite the isolation of the main glass industry. The glass furnaces in Venice itself, however, could not be less than fifteen paces from any dwelling place in case of fire. The export of glass-making materials and of cullet or broken glass was forbidden and the elaborate guild system, under the patronage of St Antony Abbot, was expressly designed to prevent the establishment of rival glass industries outside Venetian control. Members of the Aristocratic families of Venice were allowed to marry the daughters of glass-makers, and the glass-making trade was regarded as being of social importance.

These regulations were not entirely successful, however, and, as early as the thirteenth century, glasshouses were established in Bologna and in Ferrara. With the advent of the Renaissance and with the breakdown of many of the political and social factors of Medieval Europe, trade domination on this scale was not feasible, and, in the sixteenth century, Venetian monopoly was successfully broken. Nevertheless, Venetian influence on the European glass industry lasted until well into the seventeenth century, and the use of Venetian methods and of Venetian patterns was in practice for a very long time.

Very little is known about the early glass vessels produced in Venice and it is difficult to ascribe any accurate date to pieces made before the fifteenth century. Jugs, carafes and breakers would probably have comprised the bulk of the output.

After the destruction of the Syrian glass industry, and encouraged by the spirit of the Renaissance, glass-makers were able to develop Venetian production on a far wider scale than would have been conceivable at an earlier period. Stimulus given in the Renaissance to production of objects of purely secular use, rather than of those for entirely ecclesiastical purposes, as in the previous centuries, enabled the Venetians to create a series of magnificent and splendid glass vessels, which represented part of the artistic genius of Renaissance Europe.

Venetian glass metal was soda-lime, a light and thin-walled glass containing quartz-like pebbles from the river beds of northern Italy, mainly from the Ticino. The metal differed from that used in the ancient world, where sand was the predominating factor. When the silica obtained from the pebbles was fused with an alkali obtained from plant-ash and produced by burning certain plants common to the shore and salt-marshes, the result was a ductile metal that was easily manipulated and capable of elaboration with the use of tongs and pincers.

Because Venetian trade was so widespread, raw materials were not hard to come by, and soda-ash for the production of glass was imported in large quantities from Spain, as *barilla*, or as *roquetta* from Egypt and the Near East. This ready supply of raw materials, a factor of constant concern to the early glass-makers, was a further reason for Venetian dominance and enabled the establishment of a stable industry.

The Venetians also added more lime to that already included in the soda-ash, in order to strengthen the metal. Powdered marble and crushed seashells were introduced for the same purpose, and manganese was used as a de-colourising agent in order to dissipate the green tint resulting from the presence of iron in the silica, a process known to the Romans. It was the development of such technology that enabled the Venetians to produce the finest glass in the world in the fifteenth century and established Venetian supremacy in glass-making for nearly two hundred years.

Glass became one of the most elaborate and fantastic art forms of the age and in the superb and richly decorated glass vessels of the fifteenth century, the splendour and glory of the Italian Renaissance is immediately obvious.

Venetian glass of the Renaissance was heavy and massive in shape, despite the fragility of the metal, and forms were derived directly from those common to contemporary silver or to ceramics, with some use of ribs, in imitation of Roman glass. Few drinking vessels of this period have survived and a love of colour and heavy enamel decoration are typical of the period, the use of decorative motifs in enamel being closely related in inspiration to that of contemporary decorative art.

Before the seventeenth century, Venetian glass-makers made the finest coloured glass in Europe and coloured glass was the dominating feature of fifteenth-century Venetian manufacture. Blue, green, purple, turquoise (of which few pieces are known) and an opaque white glass were all developed in fifteenth-century Venice. Some coloured glass was made in imitation of semi-precious stones, following the Roman and medieval tradition of an interest in precious stones and in a love of strange and exotic markings and colour. Onyx, agate and chalcedony, known as *calcedonio* or *schmelzglas,* were all imitated by Venetian glass-makers of the period.

Opaque white metal, *lattimo* or milk-white glass, was used in the first recorded experiment in the manufacture of porcelain in Europe. This unsuccessful endeavour was made in Venice in 1470, when Maestro Antonio di S. Simone experimented in the manufacture of porcelain, using *lattimo* as one of the constituents.

Plain and undecorated surfaces were never popular in the fifteenth century. The use of enamel ornament on coloured glass was probably developed in the middle of the century and is closely related in technique to that of the enamel decoration used by the Islamic glass-makers in the Near East. It is thought, however, that the Venetian use of such decoration was an independent development and that it was derived from the use of enamel upon metalwork.

Motifs inspired by contemporary decorative art were painted on the vessels in fusible enamels and the decoration was then fired in a small oven. The dark background of coloured glass was an admirable foil for the brilliance of the enamel colours.

The use of pictorial decoration, traditionally ascribed to the invention of Angelo Beroviero, or Barovieri, in the mid-fifteenth century, was popular. Portrait heads in profile, as in contemporary portraiture, and allegorical themes were used to embellish highly ornamental goblets, and there is a close link between the subject and decoration appearing on late-fifteenth century glass and the work of contemporary artists. Such decoration was invariably anonymous, although what is supposedly the earliest decorated vessel of this kind, a goblet enamelled with 'The Flight into Egypt', *c* .1465 and now in Bologna, resembles the style of Antonio da Murano (Antonio Vivarini) who died between 1476 and 1484. Vivarini was the son of a master glass-maker and this decoration is probably his work.

The fashion for pictorial enamelling did not last long, and by the turn of the century, it was being replaced by coloured spots of enamel, and the use of simple decorative motifs painted on a clear ground, as in Islamic glass. Coloured spots of enamel, which had been used with pictorial ornament to imitate the pearls and semi-precious stones common to goldsmiths' work of the fifteenth century, now formed part of a pattern, in which they were combined with light gilding on a transparent metal, a style of ornament in fashion until about 1550.

Armorial enamelling was greatly in demand during this period and was a common feature of decorative ornament produced for the export trade. Glass with such decoration was made to order, in particular for the German market, where such work was highly prized. In about 1550, some use was also made of painted and unfired oil colours, cold work or decoration *a freddo,* particularly after the abandonment of fired enamel. This fashion was impracticable and short-lived, although it was used to decorate glass with reproductions of contemporary prints, often after the work of Raphael. Like fired enamelling, it was a decorative technique rarely practised after the mid-sixteenth century.

The Venetian glass industry of the sixteenth century reached its greatest height in the creation of new techniques and forms of decoration before 1550. The Venetians, although attempting neutrality, were constantly under pressure from the threat of Turkish ascendancy and this created considerable financial difficulty over the provision of necessary defence and of extended fortifications. The territorial expansion of Venice was now ended and financial problems became a prime consideration. Such an environment greatly stimulated the increasing production of glass, which provided the Venetian economy with a constant supply of ready financial aid.

The glass-makers achieved enormous prosperity and with their increased production and export trade, dominated the field of glass manufacture in Europe until the middle of the century. The ever-increasing European market for luxury goods was supplied with a constant flow of fantastic and fanciful glass vessels, reflecting the splendour and distortion of contemporary Mannerism.

The technical skill of the Venetian glass-makers enabled them to produce a wide range of extravagant luxury objects. Dependence upon contemporary forms of metal work or of ceramics gradually gave way to the development of more suitable shapes for glass metal. Surface decoration of the kind fashionable in the fifteenth century was virtually abolished, except for the decoration of goods produced for export, and the use of coloured glass was abandoned in favour of *cristallo,* a clear and transparent metal which was thought to resemble rock crystal, one of the greatest art forms and status symbols of the age.

Cristallo, which bore no resemblance whatever to the lead crystal glass developed in England in the late seventeenth century, was probably discovered in the mid-fifteenth century by the Barovieri, or perhaps even earlier, and was in production before the great expansion of the sixteenth century. It was transparent and was of greater clarity than any contemporary metal. The glass was refined with manganese, so making it colourless. The early *cristallo* of the fifteenth century was often pale grey in appearance, but in the sixteenth century the glass was blown more thinly and the grey colour was eventually dissipated. *Cristallo* was used in the production of the most famous and sought-after glass vessels in Europe.

The widespread use of *cristallo* enabled the glass-makers to create the fantastic forms desirable in the period. Because of the distortion caused by re-firing, enamelling on very fine *cristallo* was discontinued and, in consequence, the decoration of this light and horny material was radically different from that of the glassware of the fifteenth century. The sale of *cristallo* was forbidden to pedlars and stall-holders.

The comparatively simple bowls, sometimes derived in form from Chinese porcelain, and the dishes and other glass vessels produced before 1550 gradually evolved into forms of the utmost complexity. Decorative borders, stems and handles, often in azure-blue metal, were used in conjunction with *cristallo* and became a feature of the period.

Fantastic objects, such as glass *nefs,* were a prominent aspect of Venetian production in the mid-sixteenth century and the desire throughout Europe for drinking glasses and other vessels led to the establishment of glasshouses on the Venetian pattern elsewhere.

Ewers, in the shape of a *nef*, a form associated with decorative salts, made in *cristallo* and with surface decoration, were designed, in the fashion of the grandiose table objects of the late Middle Ages, to represent contemporary shipping and resembled the boats used in civic processions of the Italian Renaissance. They are usually attributed to Erminia Vivarini, the daughter of Alvise Vivarini (died between 1503 and 1505), but it is also probable that they were produced in Belgium in the middle of the century, when the number of glasshouses outside Venice had increased.

The most fanciful of all the decorative processes used on sixteenth-century Venetian glass was the production of filigree glass. Glass metal with criss-crossed patterns, opaque bands or embedded opaque twists in white or coloured glass was used in the creation of an overall pattern, or as a decorative feature in surface ornament. This particular form of glass was called *ritortorti* when twisted threads were used, *reticello* in the case of a small pattern, or *filagrana* in the case of filigree. *Vetro de trina,* or net glass, was another similar form of decorative metal, but here an air trap between the crossed patterns was added. This kind of metal, often called *latticino* or *latticinio,* is recorded in 1540. It was created by placing already twisted and decorative rods around a pot and then taking them up on a gathering of clear glass, twisting and drawing out the metal, so as to form interlaced patterns of varying complexity. Such work was used for surface ornament and also in the manufacture of complete vessels. *Latticino* was enormously popular in the late sixteenth century and throughout the seventeenth, and was used extensively until the end of the eighteenth century.

A number of new techniques were developed during this period. Venetian glass-makers revived the Roman use of *millefiori,* although the Venetian practice was different from that used in antiquity, the decorative glass rods being embedded in clear glass. Ice, or crackle, glass, was another technical elaboration of great skill, although it was a comparatively short-lived fashion of the mid-sixteenth century. A roughened surface and an appearance of ice was obtained by plunging a hot glass vessel in water and then re-heating it, thus creating tension and producing a broken surface. A similar effect was caused by rolling a softened vessel upon a bed of broken glass so that the small broken pieces were fused on to the object, producing the effect of ice upon the surface. These vessels were frequently adorned with small masks, similar to those used extensively throughout Europe in decorative art of the period.

Gilding was another feature of sixteenth-century work, although it was used on a relatively small scale. Venetian gilding was lightly applied and soft in appearance, often granular and of very delicate quality. It was sometimes the only decoration and was frequently erased to allow for an engraved inscription.

Diamond point engraving, although practised in Italy from the middle of the century, was never as popular in Venice as it was elsewhere. It was rarely figurative, making use of contemporary ornament, and was of a higher quality, both in design and execution, than similar engraving produced in northern Europe.

Despite the increasing importance and growth in output of glasshouses established outside Venice from the mid-sixteenth century, the Venetian glass industry in the following century was as large as it had ever been. However, the emphasis was now on quantity, rather than on quality, despite the technical skill inherent in Venetian tradition. Technical expertise began to be an end in itself and there was a corresponding decline, both in quality and in design. The extravagance of the Baroque was emphasised in ever-increasing fantasy of form; bizarre vessels, often in animal shape, were created and elaborate stems were common to this period. Mirror glass, produced since the sixteenth century, now became an important feature of Venetian output.

Aventurine glass, probably the discovery of the Miotti family, is typical of the fanciful metals desired in contemporary Europe.

This strange metal, spangled with copper oxide and forge scales to produce a metallic effect, achieved widespread popularity, and vessels of such colourful and often lurid appearance made up a large part of the Venetian export trade.

By the late seventeenth century, however, the importance of the Venetian glass trade had declined. This was largely as a result of the expanding glass industry outside Venice, as well as the discovery of stronger metals than soda glass. Venice ceased to be the dominant factor in European production. Her political power was over by the end of the century, and her sea power was in abeyance. Long-term influence from the discovery of the trade route to the East by Vasco da Gama in 1497, the establishment of the great East India Companies of the seventeenth century, the expansion of other European trading fleets, and the shortage of timber, all helped to end Venetian supremacy. In the eighteenth century, Venice became the casino of Europe and the glass trade became a tourist attraction.

Eighteenth-century Venetian glass was almost totally imitative, with a tendency to reproduce forms common to English and German manufacture. These versions of drinking glasses, originally created in heavy and lustrous metal of a radically different quality, were unsatisfactory, both in appearance and in practical use. The light Venetian soda glass was not suited to such heavy forms or to the comparative simplicity of early eighteenth-century design. Some attempts to copy the decoration fashionable in Germany and Bohemia were made by engraving on the wheel, but the results were poor and far from effective. Venetian metal was totally unsuited to cutting, although ornamental decoration of this kind was used on the ornate mirrors and elaborate chandeliers produced in eighteenth-century Venice.

Coloured glass was still made, although it was never of the depth and brilliant colour of other European metals; such ornament as existed was weak in inspiration and poor in quality, often with unfired gilding. Floral decoration in coloured glass and the mid-century revival of *lattimo,* the opaque milk-white glass of the Renaissance, were a reflection of contemporary rococo decoration and of the manufacture of European porcelain. The use of an opaque white metal, in imitation of porcelain, was common throughout eighteenth-century Europe and the Venetians exploited this fashion with some success.

Enamelling on opaque white metal was a speciality of the Miotti glasshouse in Venice. Glass had been made by the Miotti at the sign *'Al Gesù'* from the early seventeenth century, and imitation in glass of contemporary porcelain was one of the most important aspects of eighteenth-century Venetian manufacture. Some of the Miotti pieces were marked *'Al Gesù'* or *'Murano Miotti'* and dates for such items are recorded between 1731 and 1747. These pieces, created for the tourist trade in the period of the Grand Tour, were very popular throughout Europe. Horace Walpole is recorded as having purchased a set of twenty-four plates in opaque white glass on his visit to Venice in 1741. The plates were decorated in red with Venetian scenes derived from the work of topographical artists and are probably from the Miotti factory.

In the nineteenth century, museum-inspired revivalism was prevalent throughout Europe, and this encouraged a resurgence in the Venetian glass industry. Contemporary love of ornament and of involved and derivative form enabled the Venetians to re-create the fanciful glass vessels of the sixteenth and seventeenth centuries, and the export trade expanded. Showrooms for the display of Venetian glass were established in the major European cities. Antonio Salviati, working from 1866, produced some superb versions of earlier vessels, re-creating both Roman glass and the elaborate forms of the Renaissance. Pietro Bigaglia (*c.* 1840) revived the use of reticulation, Lorenzo Radi (*c.* 1861) reproduced *calcedonio,* and Francesco Ferro (*c.* 1875–1880) worked glass with the addition of metallic oxide.

This revival, combined with the increasing importance of Venetian export, had considerable influence on European glass-makers of the nineteenth century, when bizarre and purely decorative glass vessels were produced, particularly in France and England.

In the general history of the European glass industry and its development, the Venetian influence can never be underestimated. Venetian example established a pattern, both in method of production and in the creation of form, which was closely followed by other European glasshouses from the establishment of the Venetian-inspired glass-making centres in the mid-sixteenth century until the appearance of distinctive national characteristics elsewhere a century later. It was from such Venetian-inspired glassworking that subsequent European glass industries were able to expand and to react eventually against total Venetian domination, thus establishing individual and national production.

L'Altare and the establishment of Venetian-inspired glasshouses

Before the establishment of the Venetian-inspired glasshouses of the sixteenth century, there was no serious competition in the manufacture of glass and the Venetians were able to establish complete trade domination. Apart from such glass-making centres already mentioned, which are a feature of the expansion and development of commercial activity in sixteenth-century Europe, the Venetians were rarely engaged in serious trade rivalry over the manufacture and export of glass. Before the industrial expansion of the sixteenth century, the Venetian glass trade was only in competition with that of l'Altare, near Genoa, where similar methods were in use and where vessels bearing a close resemblance to those produced by the Venetian glass-makers were made.

The glass industry at l'Altare was, however, a serious rival to Venice. Comparatively little is known about it but wares produced in l'Altare were virtually indistinguishable from those produced in contemporary Murano, because the metal and forms in use at l'Altare and in glass-making centres set up by Altarists were essentially similar to those of Venice.

Glass-making at l'Altare, as at Venice, was independent in origin and the original workers came from Normandy. It grew in importance with the stimulus given to the decorative arts by the ideas and influence of the Italian Renaissance, and by the second half of the fifteenth century, production was well-established.

Unlike that of contemporary Venice, the l'Altare Guild consisted of free craftsmen, who were not bound by state domination to remain in l'Altare and who were not forbidden to practise their trade elsewhere. In contrast with the glass-makers of Murano, workmen at l'Altare were encouraged to spread the practice of their craft and to found new glasshouses. The *Universita dell'Arte Vitreae,* formed in 1495, was a trade corporation governed by a council, and laid great emphasis on trade contacts and on the importance of expansion elsewhere.

Many Altarists went to France – to Provence, Lorraine and Normandy – and also to Belgium. But it is impossible to attribute work to Altarists rather than Venetians or Venetian-inspired glass-makers, because of the similarity of style and manufacture. The importance of l'Altare lies not in the vessels produced or in the method of manufacture, but in the encouragement given to expansion in the glass trade, in the migration of Altarists and in their resulting influence upon glass production.

The sixteenth-century establishment of glasshouses in opposition to the Venetian export trade gave further encouragement to migrant glass-makers, either from Venice or from l'Altare. As early as the latter part of the fifteenth century, both Venetians and Altarists are known to have been working in France and at this time there were viable glasshouses in Padua, Treviso, Vicenza, Verona, Brescia, Bergamo, Ferrara, Ravenna, Bologna and Ancona. The long-established glass industry of Spain was stimulated by contact with the Venetians, who obtained raw materials for their glass-making via the sea trade with Barcelona. By the late sixteenth century, overall Venetian domination was challenged, although not on a large scale, by rival glass-making centres throughout Europe.

Venetian-inspired glass was being made in Vienna in 1486, and at Hall in Tirol, where glass was superbly decorated with the use of a diamond point, a flourishing production was established in 1534. This was followed by the Antwerp glasshouse of 1541, probably the most influential and important of all such centres for the production of glass on the Venetian pattern. Glass-making began in London in 1549, and more houses were established in France in 1551 and in Bohemia in 1557. In 1569, Liège achieved considerable importance in the manufacture of glass, and the craft, as practised in Italy, spread to Innsbruck in 1570, to Cassel in 1583, and to Bavaria in 1584. There is a record of a Venetian workman being at Helsingör in Sweden in 1571 and, at the same period, an Italian glass-maker is mentioned as being in Shiraz, in Persia, thus establishing the constant migration at this time.

This migration, encouraged by the ever-expanding European market, furthered the contemporary desire for drinking glasses and for exotic glass vessels created for the purpose of display. In a period of essential flamboyance the majority of the newly-established glass-making centres, unless hindered by social or political upheaval, were able to establish themselves with comparative rapidity, and it was the growth of such glasshouses and the establishment of strong and competitive industries that weakened the Venetian glass trade.

Venetian-inspired glass made in these comparatively small centres of sixteenth-century Europe is known as glass *à la façon de Venise*. This refers to contemporary glass vessels made of Venetian metal and made on the Venetian model. In the sixteenth century, the term was used to describe a particular pattern rather than a complete output from many different sources. Such vessels were virtually indistinguishable from Venetian originals and must frequently have been categorised as Venetian. But although they were very similar in technique and in actual form to those produced in Venice, particularly to those made for the export market, they were often lacking in the creative harmony and sophistication of Muranese counterparts.

It was not until the seventeenth century that distinctive national forms and ornament were established in individual and often unique production in the glass-making centres of western Europe. From this time, the overall dominance of the Venetian glass industry fell into abeyance and gave way to the rising and ever-increasing importance of the glass industry outside the Republic.

Further reading
Honey, *Glass,* 1946.
Mariacher, *Italian blown glass from Ancient Rome to Venice,* 1961.

CHAPTER FIVE

Netherlandish glass

The Netherlands of the sixteenth century included Holland, Belgium, Flanders and the territories ruled by the Prince Bishops of Liège, and the glass industry of the area is illustrated by the drinking glasses in the Dutch paintings of the seventeenth century. It was remarkable chiefly for the use of decoration on glass vessels rather than in the creation of individual form.

Glass-making in the Netherlands developed from the immigration of Italian glass-makers in the sixteenth century to what was to become the most important European glass-making centre on the Venetian pattern, the Antwerp glasshouse, established in about 1541 by Muranese craftsmen. Records show that Altarists were working in the Liège glasshouse in 1569, and glass was being made in Middleburg and in Amsterdam by the late sixteenth century. The production in all these centres was closely allied in style and method of manufacture to that of Venice.

Before the sixteenth century, the glassware of the area defined as the Netherlands was virtually indistinguishable from that of the Lower Rhineland. Vessels in *waldglas,* often of undistinguished form and poor quality and colouring, were produced, and there was some use of applied ornament. From this ornament on crude cups and beakers and from the practice of decorating the lower part of the vessels with spots of glass, the classical stem of the *römer* was developed. The *römer* was not used widely until the seventeenth century but nevertheless the decoration on the stem came from this very early style, itself possibly derived from an oriental prototype. By the mid-fifteenth century, applied spots were drawn out by the glass-makers, thus establishing the use of decorative *prunts*.

During the period of Venetian influence, the glass production of the Netherlands was not distinguished by the creation of individual or specific forms. Ice glass on the Venetian model was made in Liège, and applied and gilded bosses, often with blue enamel spots as part of the application, were used as stem ornament.

In the seventeenth century, particularly in Holland, where independence from Spanish domination was established in 1609, there was widespread development in the glass industry and many new glasshouses were set up. The Hague, Rotterdam and Amsterdam became important centres for production in Holland and the glasshouses of Liège achieved a notable manufacture under the direction of the Bonhomme family, who had further establishments in Huy and Maastricht.

At this time the glass-making centres in the Netherlands were still reliant upon Venetian influence. Soda glass, the common metal of sixteenth- and seventeenth-century Europe, was in full production and considerable use was made of design and decor-ation inspired by the export trade from contemporary Italy. The Bonhomme family, who played an important part in tech-nological developments and the expansion of the glass trade in this area, were in the mid-seventeenth century granted a monopoly in the Spanish Netherlands for the production glass on the Venetian pattern. However, it was not until the end of the century, when experiment was made throughout Europe for the creation of a stronger metal, that Venetian domination of the glass industry in the Netherlands was finally relinquished.

The close connection between the glass industry of the Nether-lands and that of the Rhineland was still apparent in the seven-teenth century and the use of the *römer* became widespread. Elaborate and highly decorative stem forms, which were produced both in Venice and in Germany and were a reflection of the fantasy and involved ornament of contemporary goldsmiths' work, were made in the glasshouses and *flügelglasser,* or drinking glasses with winged stems, were manufactured both in Germany and in the Netherlands.

Serpent stemmed glasses were another feature of seventeenth-century glass-making in this area, but like the *flügelglasser,* they lacked the stable proportion of form and decoration inherent in Venetian work, and displayed a lack of style and sophistication. This was a common fault of northern European design in comparison with Venetian work.

The *flügelglasser* and the serpent stemmed glasses achieved widespread popularity in the seventeenth century. Serpent stems were popular in the Netherlands and are recorded as being made in Amsterdam by a Venetian, Nicolas Stua, in 1667.

The use of exaggerated and ornamental forms which had little, if any, practical value was continued into the eighteenth century. Vessels of similar type, with elaborate winged and pincered stem ornament, were re-created in the late nineteenth century at Ehrenfeld, near Cologne.

This tendency towards the exaggeration of form and towards the creation of drinking vessels of little or no practical purpose is reflected in the 'flute' glasses common to the Netherlands in the seventeenth century. Flute glasses of the more attenuated variety must have been largely decorative and cannot have been created for everyday use. The flute glass was, however, a popular and commonplace shape in less fanciful form and was widely produced during this period. Flute glasses can be seen in the Dutch paintings of the seventeenth century, which provide an accurate version of ordinary life at the time. They are featured in Dutch still-life painting and are amongst the most memorable of all the glass vessels produced in the Netherlands.

It was not, however, by the creation of glass forms that the importance of the glass industry of the Netherlands was established in the pattern of Europe as a whole, but rather in the use of engraved decoration. The glass engravers of the seventeenth and eighteenth centuries produced some of the finest and most outstanding engraving in Europe, particularly in the use of the diamond point.

Engraved decoration on a glass vessel, created by scratching a design upon the surface with a diamond point, was not unique to the Netherlands, but, as has been stated, was a decorative technique used in the Roman world and practised by Islamic craftsmen. Diamond point engraving was in use in Italy by the mid-sixteenth century and the technique spread from Venice to other glass-making centres in Europe. It was never a popular form of ornament in Italy, but was exploited greatly in the north, where there was a well-established practice of engraving on metal, which possibly encouraged engraving on glass. This embellishment was never the work of glass-makers as such, but rather of independent decorating workshops or of gifted amateurs, and the ornament reflected popular forms of contemporary decoration.

The earliest vessel known to bear dated engraving of this kind is a beaker, which has the date 1566 scratched upon it and which is thought to have been made in Austria. The first recorded piece of engraved glass from the Netherlands is dated 1581, but is decorated with inscribed work of very inferior quality in comparison with similar Italian ornament.

The first use of diamond point engraving in the Netherlands was the scratching of simple linear ornament on the glass vessel and forming shadow by hatching. This simple linear decoration was practised in the late sixteenth and the seventeenth centuries and the greatest exponents of this method in the Netherlands were gifted amateurs rather than professional craftsmen.

Diamond point engraving of superb quality, both in execution and in the use of form and decoration, reached its peak in the seventeenth century, in the hands of such gifted amateurs as Anna Roemers Visscher (1583–1651) who produced decoration in both linear and stippled engraving, using small dots to create shadow, a revolutionary and unique technique for this period and datable to one glass of 1646. She is known to have been a poet and a scholar, and specialised in the ornament of green glass *römers,* with decorative motifs derived from contemporary prints. Anna Roemers Visscher made use of naturalistic forms such as flowers, fruit and insects, and also calligraphic decoration; her work is occasionally signed.

Her sister, Maria Tesselschade Roemers Visscher (1595–1649), and Anna Maria van Schurman (1607–1678) were also decorators in this field, using diamond point engraving of the linear and hatched variety.

Another gifted amateur of the seventeenth century, Willem Jacobz van Heemskerk (1613–1692) produced superb and elaborate calligraphic ornament. A cloth merchant of Leyden, a poet and dramatist and a talented engraver upon glass, van Heemskerk used linear engraving to create stylised and sophisticated decoration, relying upon the use of a highly ornamental and flowing script.

Concurrent with the use of the diamond point, engraving on the wheel developed in the Netherlands from the mid-seventeenth century. This was a professional exercise, and its development influenced the decoration produced by Willem Mooleyser.

Willem Mooleyser, a prolific engraver upon glass, worked in Rotterdam between 1685 and 1697. His decorative work, although made possible by the use of a diamond point, was profoundly influenced by contemporary engraving on the wheel. In his style, he imitated the decoration produced on the wheel by copying the variations in light and shade. These were not easily obtained in diamond point engraving as it was virtually impossible to give depth to the scratched pattern.

Early wheel engraving in the Netherlands was not skilled but was shallow and of very poor quality, compared with the highly decorative and ornamental engraving produced in contemporary Nürnberg. It was never as popular a form of ornament in the Netherlands as it was elsewhere, and tended to rely heavily for inspiration on German work. Diamond point engraving is far more representative of the decorative art of this area.

The first piece of wheel engraving that is datable to the Netherlands rather than to Germany is a goblet of 1659 on which the design commemorates a Dutch naval victory. Naval subjects had considerable popularity in Holland as themes for decoration of this kind. The use of the wheel in the production of fine engraved ornament was, however, almost invariably the work of German workmen and not of native decorators.

From the middle of the seventeenth century, glass-making centres were experimenting in the manufacture of a stronger metal than that of the soda glass that had been used throughout Europe since the beginning of Venetian dominance. In 1673, the experiments of George Ravenscroft resulted in the production of lead crystal in England. This completely revolutionary metal, which contained oxide of lead and was therefore of a far greater strength and brilliance than that of any contemporary glass, had immense commercial possibilities and led Continental glass-makers to experiment in the manufacture of a similar metal. From about 1680, there were many attempts to create something resembling Ravenscroft's discovery.

The glass-making centres in the Netherlands were no exception in this general European experimentation. Records show that Vincentio Pompeio, a Muranese who had worked in England, was in Antwerp in 1677 and in Maastricht in 1686, and it is conceivable that he may have been involved in early attempts to manufacture lead crystal. The fact that, in 1680, the Bonhomme family in Liège engaged English workmen to produce glass 'in the English fashion' could indicate an experiment in the creation of some metal similar to lead crystal, if not lead crystal itself.

Undoubtedly, some glass metal resembling English lead crystal was produced in the Netherlands in the late seventeenth and very early eighteenth centuries, but it is difficult to establish the exact origin of many of the pieces dating from this period as the metal bears close resemblance to English lead crystal and the pieces are remarkably similar in style and decoration to contemporary and comparable English work. Throughout the latter part of the seventeenth century, England and Holland had close ties, not only through political contacts and trade, but also through the interchange of ideas and influences in the field of the decorative arts. A Dutch glass-seller, Daniel van Mildert, is recorded as being naturalised in London in 1664 and the glass industries of the two countries were closely related. The Dutch are known to have imported English lead crystal into Holland from the late seventeenth century and Dutch glass of this period shows considerable English influence.

The lustre and solidity of English lead crystal, with its oily surface and its great potentiality for the play of light, made it a perfect vehicle for wheel engraving and for the use of a diamond point. Dutch love of such decoration must have increased the number of English drinking glasses imported and encouraged development in the manufacture of lead crystal. Dutch metal and workmanship were greatly inferior to contemporary English work of the late seventeenth century, and some of the engraved commemorative glasses made to record the accession of William of Orange in 1688 may have been made in England from English lead crystal and, possibly, engraved by Dutch engravers. It is equally possible, however, that many of such commemorative vessels are of Dutch origin and may be of a Dutch metal similar to lead crystal, as those made after about 1689 show distinct signs of crizzling, a common defect in such material. Another point in support of this argument is that most of these commemorative Williamite glasses thought to be of Dutch origin do not bear English inscriptions, but are decorated only with armorial engraving.

The use of English lead crystal was widespread in the Netherlands in the eighteenth century and a significant number of English bottles and drinking glasses were imported at this time. There were agents for the sale of English glass in most large towns and the excellent surface of lead crystal was used widely for the purposes of engraving. Diamond point engraving was still of immense popularity in the eighteenth century, but was almost invariably the work of gifted amateurs, whereas wheel engraving was the product of professional decorators, usually of German origin.

Throughout the eighteenth century, the glass-makers of the Netherlands attempted to make lead crystal on the English pattern, but the resulting glass metal was inadequate. The glass was poor in colour and far lighter in weight than contemporary English glass as it was lacking in the high proportion of lead apparent in the English metal. Although modelled on the contemporary English pattern, Dutch vessels were decidedly inferior in quality, and of a poor ring.

English lead crystal in the Netherlands was manufactured in the glasshouse of Sébastien Zoude at Namur. The glass was supervised in establishment and output by an English glassmaker by the name of Bridgeman, and fired with the aid of coal. Zoude's glasshouse produced a version of English lead crystal between 1753 and 1776 and was the only factory in the Netherlands to reproduce contemporary English metal successfully.

As in the seventeenth century, German influence was predominant in wheel engraving. The most notable executant of wheel engraving in the eighteenth century was Jacob Sang, who, records show, worked on English lead glass in Amsterdam, between 1752 and 1762. Jacob Sang was almost certainly related to another renowned German engraver, Andreas Friedrich Sang, who was Court engraver at Weimar and whose son, Johann Friedrich Balthasar Sang, was Court engraver at Brunswick. Jacob Sang occasionally signed his work, unlike many German engravers of the period, and his first recorded vessel, decorated upon the wheel, is a glass dated 1736. He was an accomplished and highly skilled decorator and it is possible that he was engaged upon glass cutting, as well as in the practice of glass engraving.

Sang's most famous engraving was that of the 'Velzen' glass, signed on the base: *'Jacob Sang: fec: Amsterdam 1757'*. It is now in the British Museum. The 'Velzen' glass, an English covered goblet made in lead crystal in about 1700, was decorated by Jacob Sang for the shipwright, Willem Theuniszoon Blok, to commemorate the launching of 'Velzen'. Blok was chief shipwright to the Dutch East India Company and 'Velzen' was the hundredth vessel launched during Blok's service in the Company.

The practice of wheel engraving and German influence in the Netherlands, particularly following the Treaty of Utrecht in 1713, never gave rise to the extravagance and use of lavish ornament that is typical of German glass of the eighteenth century. The work of Jacob Sang is exceptional. The glass trade in the Netherlands was almost totally reliant upon the import of glass from England and the forms of contemporary English glass vessels were copied in a weak imitation of English lead crystal. The skilled cutting and decoration of the glass produced in Germany and England at this time had little real influence in the Netherlands, although a variation of 'gold glass' was made in the late eighteenth century, and was exhibited in London at the Society of Artists of Great Britain in 1778, by Zeuner, an artist from Amsterdam described as an artist in stained glass.

The outstanding feature of glass produced in the Netherlands in the eighteenth century lies in the superb use of diamond point engraving and in the decoration, both linear and stippled, on vessels of English origin. Again, this was rarely the work of professional decorators, but of highly skilled and gifted amateurs, who reached supreme heights in this particular field. The engraving of Frans Greenwood, Aert Schouman and David Wolff is representative of all that is finest in diamond point engraving and has rarely, if ever, been surpassed.

Frans Greenwood, the eldest of the three, was born in Rotterdam in 1680, the son of Francis Greenwood and Mary Glover, who were either English or of English descent. He is thought to have been a merchant in Rotterdam before entering the

Civil Service in Dordrecht in 1726, and he died in Dordrecht in 1761.

To Greenwood is attributed the use of stippling, a far more ambitious form of engraving whereby the design is built up from a series of small dots, produced by the use of a diamond pointed etching-needle driven on to the glass surface with a small hammer. This technique, probably the invention of Greenwood and developed by him to great effect, enabled the creation of pictorial ornament which was impossible to produce with line and hatching. Anna Roemers Visscher, using stippled decoration to produce shadow in design in 1646, was a fore-runner in the practice of such revolutionary decoration, but Greenwood was certainly the first engraver to practise total stippling.

Stippling on glass bears close resemblance in execution and in effect to contemporary mezzo-tinting; the stippled dots are used to produce highlights in the design, which is delicate and of a far greater refinement than that created by linear and calligraphic engraving on a glass surface. It has been suggested that the Dutch engravers who decorated glass in this fashion may have had in mind the effect when the drinking glasses were filled with wine, which would result in a heightened contrast of light and shade.

The first recorded decoration by Greenwood is an engraved glass of 1720, in which the decorative motifs are directly related to engravings of the series 'Balli di Sfessania', figures from the Commedia dell'Arte after the work of Jacques Callot (1592–1635). This decoration is linear with hatching used to create highlights. The first of Greenwood's stippled glasses to be recorded dates from 1722 and is one of a series of drinking glasses attributable to the period between 1722 and 1749, in all of which there is no use of outline whatsoever and in which the highlights are heavily stippled.

Greenwood almost invariably worked on English lead glass and his ornament is usually dated and often signed 'F. Greenwood fecit'. Only one engraving of a landscape is recorded from his hand. His decoration is figurative and includes portraiture, pastoral and mythological subjects, inspired by the work of other artists.

Greenwood, like so many diamond point engravers, was a gifted amateur, a painter of miniatures and a versifier. He was almost certainly the master of Aert Schouman, who was born in Dordrecht in 1710 and died in 1792.

Aert Schouman, a talented painter, water-colourist and engraver, is known to have engraved his own portrait of Frans Greenwood. He was a well-known copyist and decorator in eighteenth-century Holland and studied with the painter Adriaan van der Burgh, who died in 1733. In this same year, Schouman set up as an independent artist and teacher whose work was to be reproduced by contemporary engravers. Schouman concerned himself in a wide range of decorative projects. He produced murals and wall panels and it is recorded that he decorated fans and clock dials and reproduced armorial bearings. Greenwood's son, Cornelis, was also a pupil of van der Burgh, so it is a feasible supposition that it was due to the influence of Frans Greenwood that Aert Schouman became engaged upon the decoration of glass.

In 1749, Schouman was drawing at the Academy of Design in The Hague and in 1752, on becoming a Hoofdman of the Painters' Brotherhood, he presented a glass for the use of the Brotherhood. This glass was engraved with a diamond point. The decoration, of a half-length female figure, was executed by stippling the design in the manner of Frans Greenwood, with no use of outline and with an untouched surface to indicate shadow.

In the same year, 1752, Schouman painted a ceiling decoration for the Brotherhood, using ornithological subjects. In 1765 he visited England and, despite his short stay of six weeks, his later portraiture is strongly influenced by contemporary English work.

In the following year, 1766, when Prince William V of Orange became Protector of the Guild, he presented a glass to the Painters' Brotherhood to be used as a loving cup, engraved with a portrait of the Prince. Figurative decoration is a feature of his glass engraving, in which mythological and genre subjects were used frequently and with considerable effect.

About David Wolff, the third of the great diamond point engravers of eighteenth-century Holland, very little is known, although he is thought to have been born in 'sHertogenbosch in 1732, of a Swiss father, and died at The Hague in 1798. In his use of putti and of portraiture, derived from contemporary sources, his more decorative ornament shows the probable influence of Dirk van der Aa (1731–1809), a decorative artist who had worked in Paris and who settled in The Hague, working as a carriage painter and as a decorator in the manner of Boucher.

In the work produced by David Wolff and signed by him, c. 1784 to 1794, the outlines of the ornament are occasionally executed in stipple but, unlike the decoration of Frans Greenwood and Aert Schouman, there is very little use of light and shade. Line is never in evidence and the eyes are invariably depicted as being darkened sockets, like holes, except in actual portraits.

A manner of decoration associated with Wolff and similar in approach to that of his hand is shown on a series of decorative glasses known as *Wolff* glasses, although not the work of David Wolff and unsigned. This series of drinking glasses with stippled ornament is typical of a style in evidence between c. 1775 and the early years of the nineteenth century, and the decoration is very similar to Wolff's work.

Stipple engraving was also used extensively by other glass engravers of the eighteenth century. G. H. Hoolart, born in 1716 and a nephew of Frans Greenwood, decorated glass in this manner, using plain surface to create deep shadow in the design, and J. van den Blijk (1736–1814) also produced stipple ornament inspired by the work of Dutch genre painters.

This method of glass engraving was carried on into the nineteenth century by Andries Melort (1799–1849) who executed copies of Dutch paintings in both line and stipple engraving on sheet glass. Stippling after the manner practised by David Wolff was revived in the mid-nineteenth century by D. H. de Castro, who died in 1863. De Castro, an Amsterdam chemist and a collector of *Wolff* glasses, used acid etching together with decoration in both line and stipple, thus producing a nineteenth-century variation of eighteenth-century ornament that was in reality far removed from the methods of Wolff himself.

Diamond point engraving, whether on Venetian-inspired soda glass in a linear fashion with hatching, as in the work of Anna Roemers Visscher and Willem van Heemskerk in the seventeenth century, or with stippled ornament on English lead crystal in the eighteenth century, is the most important feature in the history of Netherlandish glass-making. The work of Greenwood and Wolff in the eighteenth century ranks with the finest decorative art of the period and it was in the field of glass engraving that the Netherlands reached its height in relation to contemporary production.

Further reading
Buckley, *Frans Greenwood*, 1930.
Buckley, *D. Wolff*, 1935.
Charleston, *Dutch Decoration on English Glass*, 1957
Honey, *Glass*, 1946.

CHAPTER SIX

Spanish glass

The manufacture of glass in Spain, frequently ignored in the study of European glass, derived in part from established Roman tradition. In common with the development of glass-making elsewhere in Europe, Spanish glass-makers were profoundly influenced by Venetian technique in the sixteenth century. This influence, together with the native and virtually peasant industry of southern Spain and the advanced production of plate-glass in the eighteenth century, gave rise to the creation of some of the most individual and unique glass forms to be manufactured in western Europe.

Roman tradition, established in Hispania since the early Christian era, resulted in the migration of glass-makers from North Africa into Spain. Some glass vessels were imported from Oriental glasshouses and from glass-making centres in Gaul and the Rhineland. The Hispano-Roman industry was developed on the traditional Roman pattern and a light soda glass, refined with manganese for transparency and clarity, was used in the manufacture of blown vessels in forms similar to those throughout the Empire.

Little glass-making took place after the breakdown of Roman civilisation and the Visigoth invasions of the fifth century. Some vessels in the Roman tradition were produced, but glass was mostly used for cloisonné jewellery, where false gems made from glass metal were incorporated with goldsmiths' work.

The Moorish invasions of Spain from 711 until the tenth century, and the peaceful rule established in Cordoba by the Umayyad ruler, Abd al Rahmann II (912–961), furthered the development of a culture similar to that of Baghdad, giving rise to a Hispano-Muslim tradition and stimulating the development and expansion of glass-making in Moorish Spain. An Andalusian glass industry was well established by the eleventh and twelfth centuries; Almería and Málaga were regarded by contemporary writers as being of considerable importance. Before the fifteenth century, there was some export to Spain from the glass-making centres of Syria and Egypt.

The development of a Hispano-Muslim tradition and the manufacture of soda glass like that used in Syrian work of the late Roman Empire and in the Muslim world, encouraged the establishment of a specifically native industry. Glass vessels produced in Andalusia after the fall of Granada in 1492 until the nineteenth century were markedly different in inspiration from those produced in Castile or Catalonia, although the Venetian example of the sixteenth century had a far-reaching influence upon glass-making throughout Spain.

In Granada, in Almería, in Murcia and in Jaén, simple blown vessels were manufactured in flawed and bubbled glass metal, related in form to the Hispano-Moresque pottery of southeastern Spain and to Syrian glass of the fourteenth century. There was further influence from contemporary metal work. In Granada – at Castril de la Peña, at Don Fadrique and in Granada itself – there was a glass industry of some importance, as well as production at Pinar de la Vidriera and at María in Almería. Glass metal made at these centres was invariably of poor quality and was never colourless, unlike the *cristallo* of Venice and Barcelona.

In the late eighteenth century, there was an attempt in southern Spain to manufacture a de-colourised metal, but this was not entirely successful. A thin, pale metal of a pronounced green or yellow tint was produced, in imitation of the more sophisticated output of Catalonia and Castile, and there was some experiment in the manufacture of ice-glass, on the pattern of sixteenth-century Venice.

The metal used in southern Spain was usually green, ranging in tonality from blue to brown, either as a result of chemical imperfection or the addition of metallic oxides. A brownish-black, a blue and an amber metal were also made, and used in the two-colour vessels common to the area.

A wide range of household objects and purely domestic hollow-ware, frequently primitive in manufacture and with an emphasis on multi-handled form, was produced in southern Spain. Disproportion and the use of applied threads and pincered ornament were common to such vessels. Heavy metal was used for decorative objects while thin walled vessels were normally plain.

In the glasshouses of southern Spain soda glass, stimulated by Venetian influence of the sixteenth century and arising from long-established native tradition, was used for the manufacture of specifically Spanish forms, such as the *porró*, a long-spouted drinking vessel common to peasant Spain, and glass toys. It is almost impossible to give an accurate place of origin to glass produced in this area, although glass metal manufactured in Castril is supposedly very yellow and glass vessels of María more massive and deeper in colour.

As well as the native and often crude production of southern Spain, Spanish glass-makers developed a sophisticated and highly organised glass industry in Catalonia and Castile and, in particular, in Barcelona. This manufacture grew to prominence by the late fifteenth century, although there is no specifically Spanish form or decoration in evidence prior to this period.

Glass was produced in Barcelona from the early fourteenth century and by the fifteenth century a profitable industry was in operation. This was stimulated by the constant sea-trade between Venice and Barcelona. It was through Alicante, in Valencia, that the Venetians obtained *barilla* or soda-ash, the prime requisite for the manufacture of soda glass.

This commercial and cultural interchange is reflected in a marked Venetian influence, both in glass technology and in the use of Venetian form and ornament. The glass vessels of Barcelona, however, lacked the proportion and refinement of Italian glass. They were heavier and an exaggerated and flamboyant version of Venetian prototypes.

During the reign of Ferdinand and Isabella (1479–1516) glass manufacture in Spain was under royal protection and encouragement was given to production by a ban on imported foreign goods. However, under the Emperor Charles V (1516–1556) foreign import was resumed. The accession of Charles V united Spain and Flanders, and the Antwerp glasshouse, founded in 1541, received Imperial patronage and the patronage of Maria of Hungary, sister to Charles V and Governor of the Low Countries from 1531 to 1555. Such patronage, together with the import of Venetian glass and of glass from Flanders during the reign of Philip II (1556–1598), provided glassmakers in Barcelona with a constant source of inspiration. From the mid-sixteenth century, when Muranese and Altarist migration was at its height, there were foreign workmen in both Castile and Catalonia, and their example was of profound importance to the further development of Spanish glass-making.

In Barcelona, coloured metal and glass in imitation of semi-precious stones was in manufacture by the late fifteenth century, and throughout the sixteenth century glass vessels of all kinds were sold to other parts of Spain. Enamelled vessels on the Venetian pattern were produced from the late fifteenth century until the beginning of the seventeenth century, in particular *c.* 1550, by which time enamelling had virtually been discontinued in Venice.

Enamelled ornament, similar in technique to that of Venice, was employed in the decoration of thick-walled *cristallo*, frequently of a yellowish tone. The enamelling in use in Barcelona was quite different from that of Venice. It was primitive in comparison and of a decidedly inferior quality, and there was little of the Renaissance imagery common to Venetian practice.

Naturalistic ornament, occasional figurative motifs, religious monograms and symbolism, and the insignia of various orders of religion were depicted in freehand, in an overall exterior decoration with unfired gilding. Vessels of this kind are extremely rare.

Unfired gilding was produced by pressing gold leaf against a form of adhesive already painted on the glass, and then drying the object in warmth without refiring it. The gilding was burnished and was used to enhance the enamel colours, amongst which green and yellow were predominant. Sweetmeat jars, together with vessels for liquids of all kinds and some liturgical glasses, were decorated very effectively in this manner.

In common with other glass-making centres of sixteenth-century Europe, the manufacture of *cristallo* was a dominant feature of Spanish production and by the early seventeenth century considerable success had been achieved. *Cristallo,* however, had been made in Barcelona since the middle of the previous century and it is conceivable that a version of it was known to Spanish glass-makers as early as the very late thirteenth century.

Ice-glass was made in Spain from about 1550 and there was some diamond-point engraving, inspired by contemporary Venetian import. Strong Venetian influence at this time encouraged imitation of Italian technique and Venetian models, and Spanish love of decoration inspired the production of *latticinio,* filigree or reticulated glass, which was still popular well into the eighteenth century.

The manufacture of Spanish *latticino, 'lo rayada a la manera de Venecia',* was similar in technique to that of Venice, but was never used in the more complicated forms until the eighteenth century. It was rarely of the standard produced in Italy. Stripes of opaque white metal were frequently used in relief and the putterns *patters* were often irregular and crude in comparison with Venetian work.

Decanters and wine glasses were produced in large numbers in the sixteenth and seventeenth centuries. Spanish craftsmen used metal moulds in the manufacture of decanters, thus producing surface decoration in relief. Such vessels, with a decorated and moulded body, were then completed by drawing out the neck from the body and by the addition of a stem in the form of a hollow knop and a foot. Pattern moulding was used in a similar way, and was common throughout the seventeenth century for the production of less exotic vessels. These were expanded by further blowing after being removed from the mould, as in the case of simple forms with ribbed moulding.

Spanish wine glasses of the period were of innumerable shapes and derived from those common to Venice and to the Venetian-inspired glass-making centres of northern Europe. They were, however, lacking in the harmony of form and decoration inherent in the Italian tradition, being heavy both in metal and design.

Cadalso, in Castile in the Province of Madrid, was another notable glass-making centre in the sixteenth century. Throughout the century, the glasshouses of Cadalso produced large quantities of good quality domestic glass, despite severe competition from Venetian import. Nevertheless, these imports provided inspiration for Castilian craftsmen, who made relatively crude versions of Italian vessels in a metal vastly inferior to that of Catalonia or of Venice. It is rarely possible to give a definitive attribution to vessels of this area, as there were several other glasshouses at the time, due to the proximity of extensive supplies of wood and of clay for the pots used in glass-making.

In Seville, the leading port for trade with the Indies and a city of great prosperity in the sixteenth century, similar glass-making took place, inspired by Venice and Barcelona. In 1577, Juan Rodríguez set up a glasshouse, where it was specifically stated that he could manufacture *latticinio*, as he came from Cadalso and had worked in Barcelona and in Venice.

In 1615, Tommaso Garzoni's book *La Piazza Universale*, published in Venice in 1585, was translated by Cristóbal Suárez de Figueroa and published in Madrid. Antonio Neri's *L'arte Vetraria*, published in Florence in 1612 and translated and studied throughout Europe until the late eighteenth century, was translated, in manuscript, into Spanish in 1676. The use of works such as these and the influx of foreign workmen into Spain encouraged production of glass vessels and of mirror and plate glass on the European pattern. Very little window glass was made in Spain, except for royal palaces, until the nineteenth century.

During the period of Venetian influence, there are records of Venetian glasshouses being set up in Spain. In 1600, Domingo Barovier, a member of a well-known family of Muranese glassmakers, is recorded as being in Palma de Mallorca and, in 1608, was in charge of a glasshouse at El Escorial. In 1678, another Venetian glasshouse is recorded in Madrid, under the direction of Antonio Pellizari, who had been concerned with glass-making in Flanders and who established a very short-lived venture in the royal palace for the manufacture of window and mirror glass.

The glass metal produced in Madrid was a coarse and impure version of Venetian *cristallo*, with common discoloration caused by an excessive use of manganese. 'Combed' work was frequently in evidence, the combed decoration being created by the application of threads of opaque white metal as surface ornament. These were then dragged into a pattern with the use of a pointed instrument, as in Egyptian glass.

In 1680, Dieudonné Lambotte of Namur (died 1683) set up a glasshouse in Madrid under the patronage of the Spanish governor of Flanders. He established himself soon after at San Martín de Valdeiglesias, near Cadalso, and this concern was in operation until about 1692 for the manufacture of *cristallo* on the Venetian and Flemish pattern.

Following this period of Venetian domination, Spanish glassmakers were still reliant upon foreign example in the seventeenth century. By the late seventeenth century, however, Venetian influence upon glass-making in Europe began to wane, and from this time and throughout the eighteenth century, the Spaniards were reliant upon French and Bohemian influence.

The accession of Philip V (1683–1746, reigned 1700–1724; 1724–1746), a grandson of Louis XIV (1638–1715), stimulated French influence on the decorative arts of eighteenth-century Spain, and royal patents were granted to promoters and glass-makers, to encourage indigenous glass-making. This patronage, and in particular the large import of wheel-engraved and gilded glass from Bohemia and Germany, had a great influence on the glass industry of the eighteenth century, when the celebrated Royal factory of La Granja de San Ildefonso was founded.

Throughout the century, the constant import of foreign glass into Spain provided an endless source of imitation and inspiration for Spanish glass-makers. Cut, gilded and enamelled Bohemian glass, French mirror glass and English lead glass were imported in large quantities, particularly opaque white Bohemian glass in imitation of porcelain.

Before the foundation of San Ildefonso in 1728, there were several attempts to manufacture good quality glass in the general European tradition. In 1690, Tomás del Burgo, a promoter of glass manufacture, established a glasshouse and, in 1712, was grated a patent from Philip V for crystal glass. His unsuccessful attempts were followed by a further patent, granted in 1718 to Jean Baptiste de la Pomeraye, a Frenchman from Saint Gobain, who, with the aid of workmen from Saint Gobain, established yet another unsuccessful concern.

The factory of Juan de Goyeneche at Nuevo Baztán, near Madrid, founded under licence from Philip V in 1720, was, however, moderately successful, although Goyeneche failed to produce lead glass of the type manufactured in eighteenth-century England. Goyeneche obtained a thirty-year privilege for mirror, window and domestic glass, during which time foreign import was forbidden in Castile and the immigration of foreign craftsmen was controlled in order to foster the development of Spanish technique and, of wheel engraving, previously the prerogative of foreigners, in particular.

Goyeneche employed workmen formerly in the employ of del Burgo and of de la Pomeraye, but the foundation at Nuevo

Baztán faced considerable difficulties from the beginning, not only because of the shortage of fuel, as the furnaces were fired by wood, but also because of the severe competition from the constant import of foreign glass, against which the embargo was never enforced. To counteract the under-selling of goods from Nuevo Baztán, a sales-room was opened in Madrid, which supplied engraved glass inspired by that of Germany and Bohemia to the home market and to Spanish-America.

Due to the increasing shortage of fuel, the Nuevo Baztán concern was finally moved to Villa Nueva, an ideal location for glass manufacture because of the access to inexpensive raw materials. Such raw materials resulted in the production of poor quality metal, however, and Nuevo Baztán ceased to function in about 1728.

Later in the century, there was an attempt to manufacture glass on the German pattern at a factory run by the Dorado family at Recuenco in the Villa Nueva region. In 1740, Diego Dorado obtained a privilege for the sale of glass in Madrid and the factory supplied the Crown with bottles and window glass. In 1788, Diego and Joaquín Ruiz Dorado set up a glasshouse for the manufacture of German glass, with the help of German craftsmen. Despite royal privilege, granted in 1798, this factory failed due to lack of financial support.

In 1728, a Catalan craftsman, Ventura Sit (died 1755) left Nuevo Baztán and set up a glasshouse at San Ildefonso in Castile, near to the Royal Palace of La Granja. At La Granja, blown mirror and window glass was produced for the royal palaces by the muff process until about 1736.

The muff process enabled small-scale mirror and window glass to be made by blowing a cylinder. The ends of the cylinder were then cut and the cylinder was split lengthwise, exposed to heat and flattened to form a sheet. In about 1736, Pedro Fronvila invented a machine on which a greater expanse of sheet glass could be produced. Fronvila's method was to pour molten metal on to a heated brass table and then anneal it in an oven to condition it for grinding and for polishing on wooden rollers. The use of this process enabled La Granja to produce the largest mirror glass in eighteenth-century Europe, the finest mirrors being reserved for the royal palaces or for royal gifts. Fronvila's process was furthered by refinements in the method of polishing, developed in the middle of the century.

Following the death of Sit in 1755, the manufacture of plate glass came under the supervision of the Irish engineer, John Dowling, who left the factory in 1783. Dowling created a hydraulic polishing machine which simplified the laborious manual process. By the late eighteenth century, the molten glass was rolled by cylinder and was annealed for fifteen to twenty days before grinding.

The grinding method in operation at San Ildefonso was manual rather than mechanical. The lower glass sheet was fixed in position and the upper sheet was rubbed against it. The upper sheet was therefore ground first, five upper plates being completed before the lower sheet was finished. Imperfect pieces were used for window panes or for carriage glass.

After grinding, the plates were polished. Large plates were polished by hand, whilst the smaller plates, still of greater size than any contemporary sheet glass, were subjected to water-powered machinery after manual application with emery and amalgro, a reddish earth. The plates were polished on both sides and the whole procedure took from eight to ten days. By the late eighteenth century, plates 398.24 cm high and approximately 242.84 cm wide could be produced.

Both Charles III of Spain (1759–1788) and Charles IV (1788–1808) patronised San Ildefonso and were supplied with mirror glass and chandeliers. Candelabra, wall sconces and candle sticks were also made and there was a lens department for the grinding and polishing of optical and magnifying lenses.

As a result of fire in the Sit period the San Ildefonso works was moved beyond the palace grounds in the reign of Charles III. Between 1763 and 1774, the factory supplied the Madrid Palace with large mirrors for the throne room and similar mirrors decorated the porcelain rooms in Madrid and Aranjuez.

Twelve- to sixteen-light chandeliers were supplied for Charles II in 1764 and, in 1782, mirrors were sent from San Ildefonso to the Sultan of Turkey.

As well as plate glass and glass for the purposes of lighting or magnification, the factory produced glass vessels. Before *c.* 1755 these were in limited production, with French craftsmen predominant. Denis Sivert is recorded at San Ildefonso *c.* 1746, as is Claude Seigne from Nevers. A few years later, *c.* 1749, the manufacture of glass vessels on the French pattern was under the direction of Antoine Berger, who was responsible for the introduction of a number of French glass-makers.

The most important development in the manufacture of glass vessels, however, took place under the direction of the Swede Joseph Eder, who is recorded as working on plate glass at San Ildefonso in 1754. Eder, a master craftsman, had worked in Amsterdam in 1739 and in 1750 and eventually directed the production of hollow-ware at San Ildefonso until *c.* 1778. Experiment in clear metal was a feature of the Eder period, and colourless soda-lime glass, with bubbles and striations and of a greenish-yellow tinge due to constitutional impurity, was manufactured. Wheel engraving was produced in the German manner and in the simpler version common to eighteenth-century Bohemia. Eder's son, Lawrence, was employed as an engraver.

By 1768, a second department for the production of glass vessels was under the direction of a Hanoverian craftsman, Sigismund Brun, who had worked for Eder at San Ildefonso since boyhood and who supervised the department until about 1791. The work produced under the direction of Sigismund Brun is regarded as typifying the output of San Ildefonso.

At this time, a feature was made of engraving, frequently the work of French craftsmen. In about 1768, fired gilding, either the invention of Sigismund Brun or a derivation of current European practice, was introduced at La Granja. Here, ornamental gilding was produced by painting a design upon the vessel with an amalgam of goldleaf and honey. The decorated vessel was then fired and the gilding burnished. At La Granja, this technique was commonly used to embellish wheel engraving, as in Germany and Bohemia, although Spanish gilding was coarse in comparison. Gilding was sometimes practised on an uncut surface and both cut and plain vessels were decorated with motifs reflecting those of contemporary art. Floral decoration in the rococo manner was in use until *c.* 1790.

The establishment at San Ildefonso and the maintenance of such an expensive royal factory caused serious financial difficulty throughout the century. The geographical position of La Granja and its distance from sources of raw materials were contributory factors to this; heavy deforestation due to firing with wood, and the payment of customs dues between each province on consignments of fuel and glass-making constituents were of great concern by the middle of the century.

Charles III was therefore obliged to allow the sale of products to the public from the *Real Fábrica de Cristales,* the department at San Ildefonso responsible for vessels rather than for mirror glass. In about 1760, sale was permitted in Madrid and a retail outlet was set up in the Puerta del Sol. This was not entirely successful as the glass was too expensive and there was considerable damage to goods in transit from La Granja. The superb mirror glass was not for public sale until *c.* 1775 and then only to the nobility.

In 1762, San Ildefonso was given further protection by a grant of exclusive right of sale in Madrid and within a twenty-league radius of the factory. Sale of similar glass was forbidden to any other concern for the period of twenty-six years. Such regulations, however, were ineffectual and throughout the late eighteenth century glass-makers left La Granja to work in Madrid.

In 1774, Miguel Jerónimo Suárez, by Royal command, translated Antonio Neri's *L'arte Vetraria*, first published in Florence in 1612, using the French edition of 1752 with the addition of Merret's translation of 1662 and of Kunckel's translation of 1671. This was translated further, in manuscript, for the benefit of non-Spanish craftsmen at San Ildefonso, and enabled the factory to experiment in coloured metals and to produce opaque white glass in imitation of contemporary porcelain and of similar Bohemian work.

Transparent coloured vessels in blue, amethyst, aquamarine and emerald were produced at this period, together with imitations of semi-precious stones as in early Venetian glass. Opaque white glass, the Spanish equivalent of Venetian *lattimo*, was made in large quantities at San Ildefonso, created from an amalgam of white sand, potash and bone ash, which became opaque on cooling. This method was preferred in Spain to the method of using oxides of lead and tin with the addition of managanese.

The factory also made enamelled vessels of similar form and decoration to those with engraved ornament. In the enamelling produced at San Ildefonso, pastel colours with black or dark-toned enamel for detail or outline were used in a technique similar to that practised in oil, so that the colours were blended to create tonal variation. Floral ornament was a predominating feature of San Ildefonso and was often used for the decoration of covered jars of typically Spanish form. This enamelling was frequently carried out by decorators employed by the Royal porcelain factory of Buen Retiro (1760–1808) and in particular by Antonio Martínez, who was working at Buen Retiro from 1785 to 1804.

By the early nineteenth century, desire for fanciful ornament of this kind began to wane, and emulation of English glass became fashionable. However, this practice was never truly effective, due to the inferior quality of Spanish metal. Neither was the political and social background of the period conducive to the continued production of San Ildefonso.

Joseph Bonaparte (1768–1844) who ruled Spain from 1808 to 1813, abolished royal privilege of manufacture in 1809. The factory and the Madrid warehouses were put up for public sale and debts were ordered to be paid. Upon liquidation, the financial situation was such that it was only possible to divide the remaining unsold glass amongst the creditors. Nevertheless, the manufacture of glass continued at San Ildefonso under private management, the products being sold in Madrid through retailers.

On the return of Ferdinand VII (1808, and 1814–1833) in 1814, royal patronage was revived and manufacture for the Crown was resumed on a comparatively small scale. This resumption of manufacture was never profitable and in 1829 San Ildefonso passed into private ownership. Production was intermittent throughout the century and the factory never regained its former eminence. The Spanish glass industry of the nineteenth century was unimportant in the general pattern of European development.

The importance of Spanish glass lies in the individual and unique forms produced in the peasant industry of southern Spain and in the adaptation of Venetian influence to Spanish taste. It was not until the eighteenth century that Spanish glassmakers were able to make a significant contribution to the development of glass manufacture, and even then the comparative geographical isolation and the small production of Spain was not conducive to a Spanish influence on glass-making in contemporary Europe.

Further reading
Honey, *Glass*, 1946.
Frothingham, *Spanish Glass*, 1964.

CHAPTER SEVEN

French glass

Until the nineteenth century, the glass industry in France was never of European importance, despite a traditional practice of making window glass. In the manufacture of glass vessels, French glass-makers followed established Roman methods until the Venetian dominance of the sixteenth century. Poor quality green glass, *verre de fougère* which was a French variation of *waldglas*, was in use until this period and only simple forms were produced prior to the migration of Altarists and Muranese craftsman.

Glass vessels on the Venetian pattern were made in Lyons in 1511, and in 1551 Henri II granted a privilege to an Altarist, Theseo Mutio, who established a glasshouse at Saint Germain en Laye. Little glass has survived from this early period. The manufacture of *cristallo* appears to have been the prerogative of Italians working in France. Glass vessels, often in a dark metal of a distinctly black tinge, were decorated with enamel colours in red, white and blue, with scrolls and mottoes used in the ornament.

Glass-making centres like these did not last long, however, although from the fourteenth century onwards the profession of glass-maker had been regarded as being one of the few trades open to men of good family. Until 1650, all French glasshouses operated under royal privilege. French metal, other than *cristallo*, was generally of poor quality throughout the seventeenth and eighteenth centuries; it followed the indigenous tradition of *verre de fouqère* and was influenced by contemporary manufacture in England and in Liège.

The most important glass-making centre was in Nevers, where glass of good quality was made between *c.* 1585 and the eighteenth century. The marriage between Ludovico Gonzaga, who died in 1595, and Henrietta of Cleves, which gave the title of Duke of Nevers to the Gonzaga, encouraged Italian glass-makers to establish themselves in France. The Saroldi or Sarode family from L'Altare settled in Nevers in the sixteenth century, beginning an Italian tradition in the glass-making of the area, of which glass toys were a feature. Toys and small glass figures were made by softening glass rods in a flame and blowing or pincering the metal, creating figures on an armature of wire. This form of manufacture was not, however, unique to Nevers and figurative work of a similar kind is recorded as being made in Paris, Rouen, Marseilles and Bordeaux.

The glasshouse in Saint Sever, founded by François Garsonnet in 1605, produced some glass vessels of quality, but French glass-makers in general were more concerned with the production of mirror glass than with glass vessels.

In Lorraine, mirror glass had been made since the fourteenth century and was a notable feature of the Muranese output. The fashionable desire for mirror glass evident in French decorative art of the seventeenth century encouraged further Venetian import and mirror-makers from Italy were in constant demand.

In 1665, Colbert established a Parisian factory in the Faubourg Saint Antoine for the sole purpose of making such glass. This *Manufacture Royale des Glaces de Miroirs* was protected by the Crown and was set up with the aid of glass-makers from Venice. It was a short-lived venture as permanent Venetian help was not available. In 1670 the *Manufacture Royale des Glaces de Miroirs* was united with another factory concerned in the manufacture of mirror glass, that of Richard Lucas de Neheu, an earlier foundation established in Tourlaville in 1653.

A patent granted in 1668 to Bernard Perrot (died 1709) in Orléans was of even greater importance as Perrot, an innovator of great skill and ingenuity, developed a process for the casting of plate glass. Perrot, who was of an Italian family, had worked at Nevers and had received a glass-making privilege in 1662. He received further patents in 1668 and 1672 and had been concerned in the manufacture of red glass and in the production of an opaque white glass in imitation of porcelain. Perrot's revolutionary discovery of casting plate glass enabled the French glass industry to produce fine plate glass on a scale unequalled in seventeenth-century Europe.

Molten glass was poured on to an iron surface covered with sand, rolled, ground and then polished with the use of an abrasive, a unique process at this time and further exploited by Louis Lucas de Neheu in a factory owned by Abraham Thévart and founded in 1688. The Thévart factory, the products of which were under the patronage of Louis XIV, was amalgamated in 1695 with another factory, founded at Saint Gobain in Picardy in 1693, as the 'Manufacture Royale des Grandes Glaces'.

In the eighteenth century, apart from the exploitation of plate glass, the glass industry in France was of little importance and was singularly undeveloped in comparison with that of contemporary Europe. The poor and undistinguished indigenous output was not large enough or of sufficient quality to prevent an enormous foreign import, particularly from England and the glass-making centres in Germany and Bohemia. Such an import was of concern, despite the establishment of factories in Lorraine, notably that of Saint Quirin in 1738. The lack of Court patronage and the subsequent need for a continuous import on a large scale did not encourage French glass-makers in the manufacture of glass vessels. In 1760 the French *Académie des Sciences*, reflecting contemporary concern as to production in the French glass industry, offered a prize for a paper on suggested improvement in the manufacture of glass, an award gained by Bosc d'Antic (1726–1784).

The suggested improvements undoubtedly encouraged the further establishment of glass factories in the latter part of the eighteenth century. In 1765, the *Verrerie de Saint-Anne* was founded at Baccarat near Lunéville, and this was followed in 1767 by the establishment of the *Cristallerie de Saint-Louis* in the Münzthal in Lorraine. The *Cristallerie de Saint-Louis* achieved considerable success in the imitation of contemporary English glass. Another important glass-making centre was set up at Saint Cloud in 1784 under the title of the *Verrerie de la Reine*. All these factories manufactured glass inspired by contemporary English glasshouses, and consequently their products were unoriginal and are difficult to ascribe to a particular place of origin.

Following this period, the sole work of originality produced in France was in the practice of cameo incrustation. Also known as *cristallo ceramie* or sulphide decoration, cameo incrustation was used to embellish glass vessels in a manner inspired by contemporary classicism, and in particular by the work of Josiah Wedgewood. Ornament of this kind, in white relief, usually made in a vitreous paste of a porcellaneous texture and, sometimes, of a porcellaneous substance, had considerable vogue in the late eighteenth century and during the period of the First Empire.

Decorative motifs, inspired from classical origin, were enclosed in the surface of cut glass vessels. Desprez, a former sculptor, recorded as an independent manufacturer in Paris in 1793, enclosed such decoration in clear glass. He was gazetted as a manufacturer of porcelain cameo in 1807, 1812 and 1813. Work of this kind had been exhibited at the Paris exhibition of 1805. By 1815 *cristallo ceramie* was well established in the factory of Desprez fils in the Rue des Récollets du Temple. Such work was usually impressed, with the name and address or part of the address of the factory, common procedure in the marking of cameo incrustation. Boudon de Saint Amans (1774–1858) patented a similar process in 1818.

Cristallo ceramie was of immense popularity and had an

Above: *Bottle, in shape of fish. Egyptian, late XVIIIth Dynasty. Length
0.141 m. Page 14. A core moulded vessel with trailed ornament. British
Museum.* Below, left: *Claw Beaker, late fifth or early sixth century A.D.
Height 0.19 m. Page 37. Blown vessel, with applied and hollow prunts
in the form of claws. British Museum.* Below, right: *Mosque Lamp,
Syrian, 1330–45. Height 0.33 m. Page 43. Lamp, with calligraphic ornament in fired enamelling. British Museum*

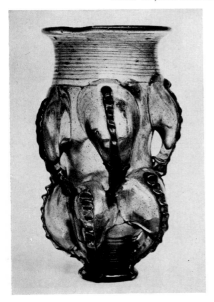

Left: *Wine glass, sixteenth century, Venetian. Height 30.48 cm. Page 54. Vetro de trina or lace glass, an elaboration of enormous complexity and of great popularity, reticulated or filigree glass being a feature of Venetian glass production until the late eighteenth century. Victoria and Albert Museum*

Right: *Goblet, second half of sixteenth century, Venetian. Height 19.69 cm. Pages 53 and 60. A typical goblet, produced both in Venice and in glasshouses of Venetian inspiration, with a large hollow and moulded knop. Victoria and Albert Museum*

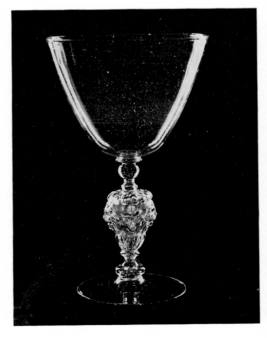

Right: *Goblet, probably
Newcastle upon Tyne,
decorated in Dordrecht and
signed 'F. Greenwood Ft.'
Height 24.2 cm. Page 71
English lead glass with a
stippled mythological
engraving by Frans Greenwood
(1680–1761), almost certainly
the first engraver to produce
a complete design by
stippling on glass. British
Museum.*

Left: *Vase,
sixteenth century, Spanish
(Maria). Height 19.69 cm.
Page 76. Flawed and bubbled
green glass, related in form
to Hispano Moresque pottery
and of ribbed form with
eight serrated handles with
pincered ornament; common
to Southern Spain. Victoria
and Albert Museum*

Left: *Vase, late nineteenth century, Nancy. Height 25.4 cm. Page 102. Layered glass with cut decoration, and signed 'Gallé'. A nature vase, with ornament derived from Gallé's botanical studies and, in particular, from his interest in the decorative art of the Far East. Victoria and Albert Museum*

Right:
Reichsadler Humpen, 1571, probably Bohemian. Height 26.8 cm. Page 108. The earliest recorded Reichsadler Humpen, with fired enamelling derived in technique from Venetian work of fifteenth and sixteenth centuries, and with decoration based on a woodcut of 1511. British Museum

Right: *Goblet and Cover, c. 1700, German (Potsdam). Height with cover 35.5 cm.; without cover 24.5 cm. Pages 111–12. Glass engraved on the wheel by Gottfried Spiller, nephew and partner of Martin Winter, director of the engraving workshop founded in Berlin in 1687. The decoration is both Hochschnitt (relief) and Tiefschnitt (intaglio). Victoria and Albert Museum*

Left: *Wine Glass, 1581, English. Height 20.6 cm. Page 118. Wine glass with diamond point engraving of animals and arabesques, 'JOHN ... JONE DIER', probably from the glasshouse of Jacopo Verzelini. Victoria and Albert Museum*

Above: *English Lead Glass, late seventeenth century. Pages 121–2. From left to right: Goblet, 1678–1681, height 16.51 cm., derived in form from a continental prototype, with raven's head seal used by George Ravenscroft; glass, height 22.86 cm., with William III sixpence, dated 1690, enclosed in the stem, and representative of the simpler forms in use following the perfection of lead glass; decanter, height 17.78 cm., probably from the Savoy Glasshouse, and decorated with pincered trailing. Victoria and Albert Museum. Below, left: Wine Glass second half of eighteenth century, English. Height 14.61 cm. Page 124. Air twist stem glass, produced after the Excise Act of 1745 and reflecting the contemporary taste for more fanciful art forms. Victoria and Albert Museum. Below, right: Bowl, late eighteenth century, probably Irish. Height 20.32 cm. Page 125. Bowl with decoration representative of Anglo-Irish cutting of the period*

Right: *Scent Bottle,
1810–20, English.
Height 7.62 cm. Pages
133–4. Cut glass
with silver gilt top,
probably made at the
glass works of Apsley
Pellatt in Southwark.
'Cristallo ceramic,
sulphide or cameo
incrustation with head
of Queen Charlotte – a
version of the method in
use by Desprez in Paris.
Victoria and Albert
Museum*

Left: *Saucer
Dish, c. 1820–40,
Eastern America.
Diameter 10 cm. Pages
145–6. Press moulded
opalescent glass of
intricate pattern common
to American glassmaking
of this period. Victoria
and Albert Museum*

Above, left: *Stiegel Flip Glass, eighteenth century, made in Manheim, Pennsylvania. Height 14.5 cm. The American Museum in Britain, Bath.* Above, right: *South Jersey Lily-pad Vase, early nineteenth century. Height 10.5 cm. Page 141. In the South Jersey tradition, unique. The American Museum in Britain, Bath.* Below: *Iridescent Favrile Glass, 1896, Tiffany, New York. From left to right: Vase, height 35.24 cm.; bottle, height 36.83 cm.; bowl, height 13 cm. Page 155. Victoria and Albert Museum*

important influence upon the work of Apsley Pellatt in England, who produced such decoration in the early nineteenth century.

It was through the glass produced in the nineteenth century that the industry began to achieve a European reputation. French glass of this period was of considerable importance in the general history of European glass-making for, not only was its production growing in industrial strength, but, in the latter part of the nineteenth century, the creation of art glass by French designers established an almost unrivalled tradition.

Manufacture in the early nineteenth century was protected from foreign competition and was furthered by the increasing use of coal, which had resulted in the practice of glass-making near to industrial centres, so that the general market expanded. Coloured glass and fanciful styles were to be made extensively throughout the century.

Such production falls into three definitive periods : that of glass made from the beginning of the century until *c.* 1830; that of an experimental and colourful period in design, between *c* .1830 until *c.* 1870; and that dominated by designers rather than by industrial production, from *c.* 1870 until the beginning of the twentieth century.

In the first period, before *c.* 1830, glass vessels tended to follow in the eighteenth century tradition of cutting and of engraved decoration. Glass of this type was largely the production of the Baccarat factory, the most important of all French glass-making concerns of the nineteenth century.

Baccarat, founded in 1765 as the *Verrerie de Saint-Anne,* was strengthened in 1816 by the addition of another factory from Vonèche. This establishment had been engaged in the manufacture of imitative English glass since 1800. The production of clear glass, with cut or engraved decoration, was a feature of the output from Baccarat throughout the century, and it was virtually the sole producer of French glass made in this fashion.

Under the aegis of Gabriel d'Artigues (died 1848) who was *Directeur* of the Baccarat factory between 1816 and 1822 and had founded Vonèche in 1800, Baccarat was able to expand production and manufacture glass on a more widespread scale. This expansion developed under the influence of Jean Baptiste Toussaint, who succeeded d'Artigues at Baccarat in 1822 and was *Directeur* until 1858. From *c.* 1835, the *Cristallerie de Saint-Louis,* which was owned by Gabriel d'Artigues from 1791 to 1797, was added to Baccarat and both the Baccarat and Saint Louis factories were run together. Baccarat's Paris depot, in operation from 1832 until 1855, had considerable influence upon the factory's production in Lorraine, as Baccarat was of great importance as an innovator in the general development of nineteenth-century French glass.

During the period of experimental and colourful vessels made between c. 1830 and *c.* 1870, contemporary Venetian and Bohemian work became of paramount importance in further development. The strong Bohemian influence at this time was reflected in the continued experiments in the manufacture of coloured glass apparent in the 1830's, and in the awards offered in 1836 by the *Société d'Encouragement pour l'Industrie Française,* for glass in the Bohemian style. Moulded and coloured glass became of particular interest from this period. French glass-makers began the production of ornamental glass vessels inspired by the highly successful and brilliantly coloured glass made in Bohemia, together with the use of the technical elaborations of the sixteenth century which had been revived in Venice from the 1830's. This revival by Venetian craftsmen of the virtuosity of the Renaissance, stimulated by the prevalent Romanticism of the period, encouraged the use of both *latticinio* and *mille fiori* work in some of the elaborate and fanciful pieces demanded by fashionable taste. Such revivalism was not, however, a true re-creation of Venetian originals, but was rather a French version of Venetian patterns, made from a totally different metal from that used in Venice.

The greatest of all French nineteenth-century innovators was Georges Bontemps (1799–1884), whose *Guide du Verrier* of 1868 was of importance in the general development of European coloured glass and who was a pioneer in the exploitation of coloured glass in France. Bontemps, who directed the factory at Choisy le Roi, founded in 1820, from 1823 until the Revolution of 1848, was able to establish a large and colourful output of ornamental and decorative glass vessels by the end of the second decade of the century. In 1827, opaline glass was in production at Choisy, followed in 1839 by a series of filigree glasses in the Ventian manner. Bontemps re-created *millefiori* in about 1844. The coloured glass of Choisy and of Baccarat was of good quality and represented the finest and most elaborate forms of French decorative and coloured glass of the period.

The Clichy factory was another important foundation. Founded as an independent industrial concern for the manufacture of cheap export glass in 1837, it was moved to Clichy la Garenne in 1844 and from this date was concerned in the production of cased and coloured glass, and particularly in the manufacture of a fine yellow metal. In 1865, aventurine glass was added to the range of metals in production. The Clichy factory was eventually absorbed into the *Verrerie de Sèvres, c.* 1885. Few of the pieces made at Clichy can be identified with accuracy, despite the large output which at one time approximated to almost a third of that of Baccarat. The contemporary reputation of Clichy was extremely high and the factory was the sole French *cristallerie* to be represented at the Great Exhibition of 1851.

Paperweights, perhaps the most immediately memorable and certainly amongst the most desirable pieces of mid-nineteenth-century French glass, reflect the desire for coloured and fanciful objects. This highly skilled invention, worked in a molten or semi-molten state, was made at Baccarat, Saint Louis and Clichy. Many copies have been made and only careful study with an expert eye can distinguish authentic examples from forgeries.

The correct dating and attribution of paperweights is not easy, but in some cases both lettering and numerals appear in part of the design. Dating on such pieces is often almost imperceptible and the dates are never centralised. No genuine paper-weight is dated later than 1849. The earliest Baccarat weight is dated 1846 and work from Baccarat is marked with B and a series of minute numerals. These almost invisible figures in red, blue or green in a cane of white opaque metal, are set in line, with the B above and between the figures 8 and 4. The Saint Louis weights, made between 1845 and 1849, are marked with SL or with a reversed S. Paperweights from Clichy made in 1849 are never dated and are marked C.

A series of extremely skilful technical methods were used in the production of an ornamental and decorative paperweight of the mid-nineteenth century. Such paperweights were elaborate and brilliantly coloured objects, often of immense complexity of design and with a unique fascination. One method of building up the pattern in paperweights was by fusing a series of coloured glass rods into a mass. In an alternative method, a single glass rod of a particular colour was dipped repeatedly into molten metal of varying tints, thus creating an elaborate design. In both methods, the resulting pattern, in the form of a multi-coloured rod, was then drawn out while still warm until the rod was of the required diameter. From this finished rod, the glass-maker cut sections in small and very thin slices, which were then polished and arranged in a complex design on a glass base. A mould was placed over the pattern on the base into which molten glass was poured and the paperweight, now consisting of three layers, base, pattern and moulded layer, was picked up on the pontil (the iron rod used by a glass-maker to hold a glass vessel during the process of manufacture). It was then dipped into more molten glass and shaped. The rough mark caused by adhesion to the pontil was ground away and the paperweight was complete.

For a paperweight of more elaborate form and decorative appearance, the pattern was covered with a layer of opaque white or coloured glass, which was later cut to leave concave depressions in the surface. Through these depressions in the overlay, known as punties, it was possible to see the underlying pattern and in a further elaboration, seen in the decoration of the rare enclosed overlay weights, another layer, usually of transparent metal, was used to cover both the pattern and the ornamental overlay.

Among the variety of patterns used for paperweights, the most important are those with naturalistic ornament, such as snakes, butterflies and lizards. The Baccarat factory produced a series of superb and highly ornamental paperweights of a wide range of designs, which included flowers, fruit and insects, and patterns in *millefiori*, in imitation of Venetian import, together with cameo incrustation and mushroom weights. The similar output from Saint Louis consisted largely of paperweights with *millefiori* ornament, whilst the Clichy factory specialised in work of brilliant colour, often in combination with the depiction of a rose.

Colourful objects of this kind were of a comparatively short-lived popularity, whereas the production of French opaline glass was an almost constant feature of manufacture until the late nineteenth century. Large quantities of moulded, opaline glass were made in all the major French factories of the period, particularly at Baccarat between *c.* 1850 and *c.* 1870, and at Clichy. Opaline glass was a product of another notable French industrial concern, the Pantin factory, which reached its height of production in about 1867.

Opaline, the term for French coloured metal of the nineteenth century, is used to describe the fine coloured glass of the period, opaque and sometimes of a heavy appearance. It is referred to in French as metal which is *opale* or which is *en couleurs opales*. It is rarely marked and is identifiable only in similarity.

In the use of opaque coloured glass, the creators of French nineteenth-century opalines reflected the influence of Venetian *lattimo*, the milk-white glass made in imitation of porcelain. The manufacture of this metal was further stimulated by the large import of coloured glass from Bohemia, where it was a feature of the *Biedermeierzeit*.

97

The simple classical forms used in the early nineteenth century were never entirely abandoned throughout the period of manufacture. Opaline glass was enhanced frequently by the addition of metal mounts. These luxury objects of comparitively simple form were made prior to *c.* 1840.

In the period between 1840 and 1870 the makers of French opaline glass experimented even further, particularly in the use of ornament. Apart from glass vessels made in the classical style, French glass-makers produced opalines of a distinctly Oriental taste, some inspired by the decorative art of the Near East and some being made in a deliberate attempt to capture the Oriental market. Turkey, in particular, was one of the most important outlets for the export of French glass. Glass vessels *à la Turque* were produced in large quantities, not only for Turkish export, but for the home market as well.

The derivation of style from Bohemian glass encouraged the production of heavy forms, and imitation of porcelain was a common feature in the manufacture of French opalines. In the period between 1845 and 1850, the glass vessels were frequently adorned with a serpent, a fashionable decorative motif of the time.

Glass of this kind was displaced eventually in the last three decades of the nineteenth century, a period marked by enormous and widespread stylistic change. Between *c.* 1870 and 1900 signed work appeared. Signed work was not always of industrial origin, but rather the creation of individual designers concerned in the production of art glass. The work such as this which appeared at the international exhibitions of the day was totally different in concept, and frequently in methods of technique, from that produced in the early part of the century, and it enabled the French glass industry to achieve almost immediate recognition in this completely new field.

The work of Joseph Brocard, encouraged by the contemporary fashion for museum-inspired revivalism in the decorative arts, was an early manifestation of the art glass of the late nineteenth century. Brocard, a highly gifted designer, was con-

cerned in the re-creation of fourteenth century Syrian enamelling. This decoration, sometimes with his signature in red
enamel, was exhibited in 1867 and was not only inspired by
Syrian enamel work but also by the decoration used on Isnik
pottery. Enamelled ornament was used by Brocard in the re-
creation of the mosque lamps produced in Syria in the fourteenth century, and such work was of sufficient quality to be
regarded as of fourteenth-century origin or ascribed to later
Venetian work for the Oriental market.

Eugène Rousseau (1827–1891) was a similar pioneer in the
field of signed glass. An artist of great talent, Rousseau was a
complete innovator in the production of glass as a purely art
form, and from c. 1875 devoted his considerable gifts to the
manufacture of ornamental and decorative glass vessels. Rousseau was not only concerned with historical revivalism, but
was deeply influenced by the inspiration he gained from the
study of Oriental art and, in particular, from Japanese design,
which was of great interest to contemporary connoisseurs. This
glass was a notable feature of the Paris Exhibitions of 1878 and
1884. At these Exhibitions, the signed work of Rousseau made
an enormous impact on fashionable taste. Such work, however, is rare. Rousseau retired from the production of art glass
in about 1885 and his work was carried on by E. Leveillé
until the beginning of this century. The signed art glass of
Eugène Rousseau is marked by an engraved signature with
a gold flourish, whereas there is no mark of origin upon the
similar individual work produced by Leveillé. However, some
work carried out by Leveillé, under the aegis of Eugéne Rousseau, bears the inscription *'Rousseau-Leveillé'*, together with
the address of Leveillé at 74 Boulevard Haussmann, inscribed
in diamond point engraving.

The enamelled ornament of Brocard and the art glass of
Eugène Rousseau were of great importance to the artistic development of Emile Gallé, the most influential figure in the
creation of French decorative art glass of the late nineteenth
century.

Emile Gallé (1846–1904) was born in Nancy, the son of a dealer in pottery and glass. He attended the Art School at Weimar and studied glass-making at Miesenthal. This early training in the fields of design and industrial practice enabled Gallé to achieve an artistic and technical perfection in his work which has seldom, if ever, been surpassed. He was a brilliant innovator from the point of view of design and in the development of industrial and technical methods.

Gallé was a man of diverse interests and eclectic genius and a serious and scientific botanist of some repute. He was a chemist and above all, a designer of extraordinary and outstanding talent, who was later to dominate the Ecole de Nancy, the leading centre for the creation of Art Nouveau in France.

Like Rousseau and other leading artists of the day, Emile Gallé reflected in his work the profound influence which came to the European decorative arts from Japan. The study of Japanese art had an important effect upon the work of Gallé and this influence, combined with his intense love of naturalistic ornament derived in part from his botanical studies, enabled him to create a series of diverse and unique art forms in glass. He was, however, not solely concerned with the manufacture of glass vessels, but was also instrumental in the design and manufacture of both pottery and furniture.

In his early work, Gallé used the enamelled ornament pioneered by Joseph Brocard in the revival of fourteenth-century Syrian enamelling. This period in his career was marked by constant experiment and enamelling was only one of the technical methods in practice. Ornament inspired by the work of Brocard, animal motifs, floral decoration and endless experiments of one kind or another typify the work of Gallé in the 1870s, a period of intense discovery and of great importance to his later development.

In 1878, the Gallé display at the Union Centrale Exhibition in Paris aroused considerable public interest. In particular, his *Clair de Lune* glass was admired greatly. This effective and highly decorative glass metal was a conscious reflection of his interest in the art of the Far East. It was inspired by an eighteenth-century Chinese glaze, and concurred with the contemporary taste for all that was oriental. It was immediately successful. Such an outstanding metal was created with the use of potassium and cobalt oxide and was of a unique and beautiful blue, which, by virtue of the constituent, changed in colour if exposed to a strong light.

In the same year, 1878, partly as a result of his sensational display at the Paris exhibition, Gallé was able to expand his commercial concern in Nancy and to build extensive furnaces and decorating workshops.

From this period, the Gallé production grew in strength and at the *Exposition des Beaux Arts* in 1884, a wide range of luxury art glass from Nancy was exhibited. The most important exhibits were not of *Clair de Lune* glass, but were of amber or smoke-like metal decorated with naturalistic ornament. In the following year, 1885, as part of the general expansion in commercial enlargement and increased production, the Paris shop, *l'Escalier de Crystal*, was able to display a range of highly influential and unique table glass designed by Gallé. This Parisian outlet for the manufacture from Nancy furthered the already considerable reputation of his work.

It was, however, the Gallé display at the Paris Exhibition of 1889 that excited the most interest in his art glass. Here, unique vessels, which would rarely, if ever, be repeated on a widespread scale, were on view. Such vessels, individual forms created for wealthy and discriminating connoisseurs, were almost invariably pieces of cased glass. This method of casing glass, as used in the Portland Vase, was constantly in operation in Nancy and was endlessly exploited by Gallé, either in the form of *verre doublé,* in two layers, or occasionally, as *verre triplé,* in three. For the Exhibition of 1889 he created cased glass with a dark overlay, in either brown or black metal, on a transparent ground. *Verre doublé,* carved in imitation of hard-stones, was referred to as *noir* or *hyalite* in the case of the black overlay, and was used in the creation of glass forms normally manufactured in limited numbers and comprising a unique series.

At about this time, Gallé opened a shop in Frankfurt, and despite a rapid expansion of trade and an almost constant demand for decorative glass, the industrial manufacture at Nancy achieved a very high standard of technical production.

From 1889, the growing influence of Art Nouveau and the corresponding interest in naturalistic and plant form were further exploited by Gallé to superb effect. The nature vases, possibly his most famous creations, date from this period. Glass vessels of magnificent quality, both in design and technique, were now produced at Nancy, either in the form of unique presentation pieces or in limited series, or as commercial series using a variety of forms with uniform decoration. These pieces were coloured, cased and decorated with naturalistic ornament and motifs inspired by Gallé's studies of pond and marine life, and reflected his interest in oriental art and, in particular, his love of Chinese art of the eighteenth and nineteenth centuries. It was in the period following 1889 that the inventive and eclectic genius of Gallé was at its height and his art glass, in sympathy with the aims and ideals of Art Nouveau, surpassed any other of the period.

The Art Nouveau vases produced in the 1890's are frequently difficult to date with complete accuracy, particularly the Nature series, because of the extraordinary popularity of art glass in this form. Another range of similar vessels, the *Paysages de Verres* series, was a further reflection of the profoundly oriental taste of Gallé. The paramount influence of oriental lacquer was a dominant feature in the series produced at this time.

Marqueterie de verre, created by Gallé in 1897, was a technique of even greater elaboration than that used in all the preceding series. This highly skilled form of ornament was produced by pressing semi-molten metal on to a warm body, and then carving a decorative surface so as to achieve the effect of marquetry similar to that in use upon furniture. Such a complicated process, however, was not completely effective and the vessels were rarely flawless. Vases of *marqueterie de verre,* often of fantastic and abstract form, were frequently enhanced by the addition of elaborate mounts made by the leading silver-smiths of the day. These exotic vases were never in large scale production and were collectors' items of superb quality.

By the time of the Paris International Exhibition of 1900, the Gallé concern in Nancy was employing three hundred craftsmen. Contemporary desire for cut-glass led to even further increase in production and, to satisfy commercial demand, some use of hydrofluoric acid was made. Hydrofluoric acid accelerated the cutting process, so enabling cased vases to be created with greater rapidity and in larger numbers. Two-colour vessels in *verre doublé* were dipped in hydrofluoric acid. The decorative surface, covered with an acid resistant, was then finished on the wheel with naturalistic ornament. Lamps were an important aspect of Gallé's industrial production.

Emile Gallé died in 1904 but the Nancy factory remained in operation until 1935. Art glass made after his death was usually of *verre doublé* with acid cutting on a frosted and unpolished ground.

Gallé was one of the first designers to mark glass and his creative life lasted longer than those of any of his contemporaries of the late nineteenth century. The Gallé concern in Nancy was not only involved in the manufacture of individual pieces and of limited series, but was in production for commercial vessels, and consequently there is considerable difference in the marking used at Nancy from one period to another.

In the 1880s, vessels produced by Gallé were marked *'Emile Gallé'* or *'E. Gallé'*, sometimes in conjunction with 'Nancy' or the Cross of Lorraine. Another mark used at Nancy was that of *'Cristallerie d'Emile Gallé, modèle et décor déposé'*. *'E. Gallé Fecit'* or the very rare *'E. Gallé Comp.'* were also in use. Marks like these were invariably executed with thought and were unobtrusive, painted or incised on the base of a vessel or placed under a motif in the enamelled ornament. Nature vases bore a different mark from that appearing on enamelled glass; *'Gallé'* in relief or as an incised inscription. In conjunction with the invariable derivation from designs of the Far East, a simulation of oriental calligraphy was practised for the inscription. Dated pieces were made for the various Paris Exhibitions and the series of vases inspired by oriental lacquer-work in the last decade of the nineteenth century was marked with an impressed stamp. Later art glass, partially created by the acid process, was marked *'Gallé Déposé'*. After Gallé's death a similar signature to that practised in his lifetime was used, but this cursive inscription was etched upon the vessels in relief. The same inscription, used in conjunction with a star, was used between *c.* 1904 and *c.* 1914.

Apart from the Gallé manufacture, acid-cut glass was produced at the Dum factory in Nancy, which was in operation from 1875. Orange and yellow metal were frequently in use in the Dum production.

The work of Emile Gallé, displaying the technical virtuosity and wide range of his inventive genius, established a pattern in the creation of French art glass of the finest quality. Such decorative and ornamental glass became a feature of French manufacture of the twentieth century and is exemplified in the work of René Lalique, 1860–1945, whose career as a designer of glass is outside the range covered in this book.

Further reading

Amic, *L'Opaline Française au XIXe Siècle*, 1952.
Barrelet, *La Verrerie en France*, 1953.
Dennis, 'Gallé in *Antiques International*, 1966.
Hollister, *The Encyclopedia of Glass Paperweights*, 1969.
Honey, *Glass*, 1946.
McCawley, *Antique Glass Paperweights from France*, 1968.
Polak, *French C19 Glass*, 1961.
Polak, *Modern Glass*, 1962.

CHAPTER EIGHT

German and Bohemian glass

The glass of Germany and Bohemia is peculiarly distinctive when compared with the work of Europe as a whole, but because of their close proximity, the production of the two areas was very similar.

The forests of Germany provided vast sources of raw material and glass was made in the forest country east of the Rhine, in Hesse, in the Reisengebirge, on the borders of Bohemia and Silesia, in the Böhmerwalde on its Bavarian side, and in Saxonia, Thuringia and Franconia. German glass production, however, was not fully exploited until the sixteenth century, when Muranese influence led to a widespread production of glass on the Venetian pattern, in conjunction with many forms of specifically Teutonic origin.

Prior to the sixteenth century, German glass derived from the Teutonic glass made after the collapse of the Roman Empire and before Venetian dominance became apparent. The glass metal was different from that of soda glass : it was usually greenish in colour and of imperfect quality, The metal was made with plant ash and was known as *waldglas* or forest glass, and relatively crude forms were made in green, yellow and brown. These imperfect and often poor quality vessels were usually made without feet and were decorated with simple, applied ornament.

In the general history of German glass-making, forms peculiar to Teutonic glass appear, as well as others, like the Römer, which were not only produced in Germany but also in the Netherlands. Unique Germanic shapes were made in Germany during the Venetian period at the same time as drinking glasses modelled upon those of Venice. In the Venetian glasshouses, vessels for the German market were made to German order and on a Germanic pattern as part of the sixteenth-century export to Germany.

The most important of the German drinking glasses was the *Römer*, a product of northern and north-western Germany, which had immense popularity throughout northern Europe, particularly in the sixteenth century. The *Römer* was a wide-mouthed drinking glass, with a large globular bowl and a straight stem decorated with applied ornament. The decoration was derived from that used upon Roman vessels and from the practice of applying spots of glass (or *prunts*) to cups and beakers. In the mid-sixteenth century, these applied spots were drawn out in points or impressed. Such impressed forms are referred to as *raspberry prunts*. The domed foot, a feature of the *Römer*, was made by winding a glass thread around a removable core of wood or of metal, but, later, it was common practice to use a blown foot with an applied thread.

Apart from the *Römer*, which was the most popular drinking vessel and was made for a longer period of time than any other German drinking glass, glasses of massive shape and size were produced in Germany for the relatively unsophisticated society of the time. These glasses were totally different in conception from those required for a more sophisticated taste. They were cylindrical and were not only massive in shape and size, but often of a greater height than other contemporary glass objects. They were created for convivial and communal purposes and were occasionally marked in sections for the purposes of competitive drinking. Of the very large cylindrical glasses, the two most popular versions were the *Willkom* and the *Humpen*, a variation of the *Willkom*, both of which were vehicles for decoration in enamel. The *Stangenglas*, or pole-glass, was adorned frequently with prunts, while applied rings were used to denote the sections of the *Passglas,* which was for communal drinking. The love of strange shapes, together with the crudity of taste, led the glass-makers to make many trick and puzzle glasses of one kind or another. The *Kuttrolf,* or *Angster,* which was a vessel with several twisted necks and one mouth, was another very popular German glass form and was used for sprinkling or for pouring liquid very slowly.

In the sixteenth and seventeenth centuries, when the influence of Venice was predominant throughout Europe, German glass gradually became more sophisticated both in manufacture and in appearance and, although specific German shapes were in use, the inspiration from Venice gave rise to several distinctive forms of decoration.

The earliest and most important of these decorative forms was the use of the Venetian-type enamelling. Coloured glass was ground to powder and, after being mixed with a binder, was painted on to the vessels and then fired to achieve a highly decorative effect. Like the Venetians, the Germans rarely used oil or lacquer colours in their decoration, although they did occasionally produce unfired work. German enamelled glass can hardly be given an accurate attribution regarding place of origin, as it was a popular art utilising decoration and ornament universal throughout Germany.

Before the middle of the sixteenth century, German vessels were usually undecorated, except for applied or moulded ornament, but imported commissioned glass from Venice was a fashionable luxury. German enamelled decoration, as such, modelled on the Venetian original and carried out on Venetian-inspired metal, did not appear until the mid-sixteenth century, when glass vessels were given armorial ornament, and figurative themes were not in use until *c.* 1570.

The figurative decoration on German glass was not distinguished or very original. It was based upon contemporary woodcuts and engravings and was closely related in inspiration to popular folk art. The vessels were often decorated by skilled itinerant craftsmen and in the late sixteenth and early seventeenth centuries the enamelled ornament was commonly Bohemian in origin rather than specifically German. Cobalt blue glass, a feature of the Bohemian glass industry, was a popular ground for such decoration.

Glass decorated with armorial bearings, portraiture, Biblical, satirical and allegorical themes, representations of workers and trades, possibly for presentation to members of the represented guild, and innumerable decorative themes of one kind or an-other are known. The most famous of these enamelled decorations was that used upon the *Reichsadler Humpen,* a large cylindrical glass vessel decorated with a *Reichsadler,* the double-headed Imperial eagle, together with the shields of an idealised version of the constituents parts of the Holy Roman Empire. The earliest version of this design is a woodcut of 1511, although the first *Reichsadler Humpen* to be recorded is the vessel dated 1571, now in the British Museum. Another very popular form of enamelling was that of the *Kurfürstenhumpen,* on which the decoration represented the Holy Roman Emperor and the seven Electors. Such designs were usually derived from a seventeenth-century print by Hans Vogel of Augsburg, although the first recorded decoration of this kind dates from 1591.

This type of enamelled ornament, virtually peasant art in relatively poor quality opaque enamel colours on almost colourless glass, was highly popular for a considerable period of time and decorative glass of all kinds was a feature of German and Bohemian glasshouses.

In the seventeenth century, enamelled ornament was produced for the German Courts as well as for popular and more mundane decoration, and vessels of this type were usually dated and initialled. Such vessels, known as *Hofkellerei* glasses, were embellished with the armorial bearings of various princely owners. Of particular note is the glass produced for the Court of Saxony which was decorated with the arms of Poland after the Elector Freidrich Augustus the First

(Augustus the Strong, 1670–1733) became King of Poland in 1697.

There was further development in the decoration of glass in the seventeenth century, when painting in black, *Schwartzlot,* with the occasional use of red and gold and with needle-scratched detail, became a feature of German work. *Schwartzlot* decoration was derived from that of domestic window glass, and Johann Schaper, born in Hamburg in 1621, produced superb work of this kind. Schaper, originally a painter of stained window glass, was a *hausmaler* or decorator, working on his own account on both glass and faience, and is known to have worked in Nürnberg from 1655 and to have been in Ratisbon in 1664. He died in 1670. The *Schwartzlot* decoration created by Schaper is closely related in style, although not in technique, to the engraving tradition in Nürnberg, a city famous for engraving and for goldsmiths' work.

Schaper's pupil, Daniel Preissler (1636–1733), like his master a decorator of unadorned glass vessels, Preissler's son Ignaz, who worked in Silesia and Bohemia, and Abraham Helmhack (1654–1724) all produced *Schwartzlot* decoration. Eighteenth-century enamelling tended to follow the widespread European fashion for decorating opaque white glass in a manner designed to make the objects resemble contemporary porcelain. Bohemia was the main source of such work and helped to boost the export of decorative glass.

Until the late seventeenth century the use of Venetian form, stimulated by the Italian export trade, remained. This influence was eventually displaced by the growing importance of a much heavier metal. The use of potash and chalk *c.* 1680 enabled German glass-makers to manufacture a metal of greater brilliance and of more massive appearance, revolutionary in every way from current practice in Germany and in Bohemia. Such development gave rise to experiment in new forms, thus destroying Venetian domination. Potash-chalk glass was lustrous and heavy and eminently suitable for decoration by cutting, or by engraving with the wheel, and its discovery aided the production of cut and engraved glass on a far more widespread scale than had been possible at any time before.

As a result of this development, cutting and engraving on glass using a copper wheel became one of the most important aspects of production and was a feature of Baroque and Rococo ornament. This laid the foundation for the great eighteenth-century glass industry of Silesia and Bohemia, although both cutting and wheel engraving had been used before *c.* 1680.

The art of engraving glass on the wheel was known to the Romans. It was practised by Islamic craftsmen and engraved rock crystal was one of the great art forms of the sixteenth and early seventeenth centuries. Casper Lehmann (*c.* 1570–1622) was almost certainly the first European artist to work on glass in this manner and was probably trained as a glass engraver by Valentin Drausch, a stone-cutter from Strasburg, who had come to Bavaria, *c.* 1570, to work with the Fontana or the Saracco, rock crystal cutters from Milan. Lehmann, from Ulzen in the province of Luneburg, is recorded in Prague in 1588. He was granted a title of nobility and a monopoly for the production of engraved glass, and was created Imperial Court glass and hard-stone engraver to the Emperor Rudolf II, a great patron of the arts. He may also have worked in Dresden from 1606 to 1608. Georg Schindler is recorded as having worked in Prague as a glass cutter in about 1610. Decorative cutting became fairly well established in the reign of Rudolf II (died 1612) and spread to Bohemia, Saxony, Thuringia, Munich and Nürnberg.

On Lehmann's death, his privilege was bequeathed to his pupil, Georg Schwanhardt (1601–1667), who returned to Nürnberg in 1622. Schwanhardt founded a school of glass engravers in Nürnberg which included his two sons, Georg Schwanhardt, died 1676, and Heinrich, who died in 1693, and his three daughters, Sophia, Maria and Susanna. Schwanhardt polished some of his engraving and used a diamond point to enhance some of the detail. His son Heinrich is credited with pioneering the use of acid as a method of etching on glass, a process exploited with great effect in the nineteenth century. Hermann Schwinger (1640–1681) and Georg Friedrich Killinger, died 1726, also practised wheel engraving in Nürnberg, which was one of the wealthiest and most prominent cities of Germany and an artistic centre of considerable importance. Engraved and cut decoration of the Nürnberg school was used to embellish shapes derived from those of metalwork.

Glass engraving reached its height between 1685 and 1775. It was often the work of anonymous craftsmen and was mainly produced on either side of the Reisengebirge, in north-eastern Bohemia, and in Silesia. The most important work was done in the service of various German courts.

In 1687, Count Christoph Leopold von Schaffgotsch granted a privilege to Friedrich Winter (died 1702) for the engraving of glass in the manner of rock crystal, and in *c.* 1690 the Schaffgotsch Mill was set up under his patronage at Petersdorf in Silesia. It was driven by water-power and produced *Hochsnitt* or cameo work. In 1687, the same year as Winter's privilege, another water-powered mill was set up, under the patronage of the Elector Friedrich Wilhelm of Brandenburg, who in 1679 had established a glasshouse directed by Johann Kunckel in Potsdam. Kunckel (1630–1703) who worked in Potsdam from *c.* 1679 uncil *c.* 1690, was a chemist of note who published a book, *Ars Vitraria Experimentalis,* in 1679, based upon that by Antonio Neri published in Florence in 1612. In the same year or thereabouts, he developed a ruby-coloured glass with the use of gold chloride, a discovery originally made by Andreas Cassius. Green, blue and agate glass were made in Potsdam, although coloured glass was also made elsewhere in Germany and was engraved on the wheel in the late seventeenth century. By 1689, Kunckel was using chalk in the manufacture of glass, thus creating a superb vehicle for engraving. The Potsdam glass was prone to crizzling, or to incipient decay, a common defect in experimental metal in the seventeenth century.

In 1687, in association with the Potsdam glasshouse of 1679, an engraving workshop was set up in Berlin. It was a water-powered mill under the control of Martin Winter, the brother of the Friedrich Winter who had been granted the Schaffgotsch privilege. Martin Winter had been employed by the Elector of Brandenburg since 1680. He died in 1702. The mill was intended for the production of *Hochsnitt*, although *Tiefschnitt*, or intaglio work, was produced at the same time. Martin Winter's nephew, Gottfried Spiller, who had been his partner since 1683, also worked in Berlin, as did his contemporary, a Bohemian called Heinrich Jager, who was working in Berlin *c.* 1700.

The heavy tankards and goblets with domed covers and the massive pieces decorated in Potsdam were sometimes gilded and very often decorated with military scenes and later with putti. Decoration used by the engravers on the lobed goblets and short-stemmed sweetmeat glasses and on the lobed, scrolled and shell-shaped forms of the eighteenth century included armorial bearings, figurative and topographical engravings, allegorical figures, flowers, scrolls and miniature landscapes, and was derived from contemporary sources.

The greatest German glass engraver of the late seventeenth and early eighteenth century was Franz Gondelach, born in Hesse in 1663, who was working for the Landgrave Karl of Hesse-Cassel in 1695. Gondelach sometimes worked on Potsdam glass and his son-in-law, Johann Franz Trumper, is recorded in Berlin in 1717–1718.

Apart from work produced in Silesia and Potsdam and the work of Gondelach in Hesse, glass was engraved in Bohemia, and in Nürnberg by Johann Heel (1637–1709), an engraver and silversmith who had decorated faience. Anton Wilhelm Mäuerl (1672–1737) produced some signed work, as did G. E. Kunckel in Thuringia. Three members of the Sang family from Ilmenau, Andreas Friedrich Sang, recorded in Weimar 1720–1744, Johann Heinrich Sang, his son, recorded as a glass engraver in Brunswick, and his brother, Jacob Sang, who is known to have worked in Holland, signed decoration of this kind, and Christian Gottfried Schneider (1710–1773) from

Warmbrunn, working after 1725, is another named decorator. Signed work, however, is exceptional.

Engraved glass was also produced in Brunswick and in Saxony, where Ehrenfried Walters von Tschirnhausen (1651–1708) had been concerned in the establishment of glasshouses in Dresden and elsewhere. After *c.* 1725, however, the glasshouses in Silesia assumed the greatest importance, creating some of the most outstanding work of the eighteenth century. From this date, the Bohemian glass industry manufactured a variety of cheaper goods for the outside market and developed a large and flourishing export trade throughout Europe.

The development of Bohemian glass was closely related to that of the German glass industry and was not of any real importance until the late sixteenth century, when the popular and decorative cobalt blue glass was used as a vehicle for enamel painting. In the seventeenth century, when glass engraving became a feature of German work and there was considerable patronage of the glass industry by the Bohemian nobility, German workmen migrated to Bohemia and itinerant glass-makers and decorators travelled throughout the country. By the latter part of the seventeenth century and certainly by the early eighteenth century, there was a highly organised and successful glass trade and the suitability of Bohemian metal for engraving on the wheel helped to establish an export trade throughout Europe.

Engraved decoration on the goblets and covers, tankards, tumblers and sweetmeat dishes of the late seventeenth century tended to be crude and imitative of work done in Nürnberg, with unpolished engraving and the use of figurative and floral ornament. In the early eighteenth century, goblets and tumblers were decorated with flowers and foliage over the whole surface in a formal pattern, and towards 1720, decoration consisted of Baroque strapwork and foliate interlacing, *Laub und Bandelwerk,* sometimes incorporating small figures from contemporary decorative prints. One of the most characteristic forms to be decorated in this way was the faceted or polygonal tumbler.

Engraving on glass was, however, essentially a product of the Baroque and the Rococo, and in the late eighteenth century engraved ornament was almost entirely superseded by brilliant cut-glass in the English style. By the beginning of the nineteenth century, cylindrical tumblers and straight-sided goblets had replaced the elaborate forms of the previous period. The popularity of travel, following the Napoleonic Wars, as well as the prevalent romanticism of early nineteenth-century Europe, encouraged glass-makers to produce engraved glasses for the tourist trade; pieces engraved with views of spa towns and other topographical subjects. The portrait work of Dominik Biemann (1800–1857), who worked in Prague, is representative of the finest work of this period, and in the latter part of the nineteenth century, superbly engraved work was produced in Bohemia, in keeping with the feeling for museum-inspired revivalism common throughout Europe.

Despite the German love of elaboration, goldleaf was rarely applied to the surface of glass vessels, except in the case of Court commissions. However, between the 1730s and the 1760s, *Zwischengoldgläser*, glasses decorated in the same technique as Roman catacomb glass, were made in Bohemia. Gold leaf was applied and engraved on the outside of a glass vessel and a carefully ground outer layer, corresponding to the inner vessel, was placed over it. The two layers were then cemented together and finished with a disc at the base. This process enabled glass to be gilded, or to be decorated with silver leaf, or ruby or green lacquer, without the risk of damage through handling. Johann Joseph Mildner (1763–1808), working at Gutenbrunn in Lower Austria, created a variation of the *Zwischegoldgläser* by cutting away an oval in the surface of a vessel and inserting a glass medallion on the reverse of which was a design, often in the neo-classical manner.

Opaque white glass, with decoration resembling that of contemporary porcelain, was also produced from *c.* 1750, particularly in Bohemia where it constituted a large proportion of the export trade. The use of coloured and decorative glass is a feature of both the German and the Bohemian glass industries of the nineteenth century.

In Germany, Samuel Mohn (1762–1815), who worked in Dresden from 1809 and had been a painter of silhouettes, and his son, Gottlob Samuel Mohn (1789–1825), who worked in Vienna from 1811, produced decorative ornament in transparent enamel colours, as did Anton Kothgasser (1769–1851) and Franz Anton Siebel (1777–1842). After 1850, the fashion for museum-inspired revivalism encouraged the re-creation of Renaissance and Baroque enamelling. There was some influence from Islamic glass prior to the *Jugendstil*, when the work of Gallé at Nancy gave rise to the use of naturalistic forms and floral decoration, as in the work of Karl Köpping of Berlin (1848–1914).

In nineteenth century Bohemia, there was a general resurgence in the glass industry following the Napoleonic Wars and in the *Beidermeierzeit* and emphasis was laid on coloured and flashed glass. Flashed glass was popular for the manufacture of two layer vessels, where the thin outer layer was cut in a pattern to expose the main body. Ruby red, green, blue, amethyst, greenish-yellow, yellowish-green, topaz, amber and opaque white metal were all utilised at this time. The glassworks of Count von Buquoy (1781–1851) produced a heavy red glass, and in 1820 an opaque black glass was made. Both these highly coloured metals were referred to as *Hyalith*. Black glass had previously been made in Bohemia and in particular at Zechlin, where it had been produced from 1804, primarily in imitation of Wedgwood's basaltes. A strongly coloured, marbled and opaque glass, patented as *Lithyalin*, was produced at Blottendorf, *c.* 1828, by Friederich Egermann (1777–1864), a noted manufacturer of Bohemian coloured glass. These coloured and bizarre metals were greatly admired and eminently suitable for use in the creation of the massive and decorative objects of the *Beidermeierzeit*.

In the latter part of the nineteenth century, the Bohemian glass industry did not escape the widespread influence of museum-inspired revivalism. Apart from work of this kind, Bohemian glass-makers produced a wide range of cheaper wares for export, which were heavily influenced by contemporary fashion in decorative art.

Further reading

Honey, *Glass*, 1946.

Pesatova, *Bohemian Engraved Glass*, 1962.

Saldern, *German Glass*, Corning Museum, 1965.

Weiss, *The Book of Glass*, 1971.

CHAPTER NINE

English glass

In common with contemporary development in Europe, English glass-makers did not begin production of good quality glass until the sixteenth century, following the establishment of Venetian inspired glasshouses on the Continent. The English glass industry was derivative in origin and practice until the late seventeenth century, when the discovery of lead glass enabled a radical change and expansion in manufacture to take place.

Before the sixteenth century, glass in England was made in the Roman tradition. Green potash glass was manufactured on a small scale where sand and wood were available in sufficient quantities, mostly in the Weald of Kent, Surrey and Sussex. Some window glass was made, but was inferior to foreign manufacture, which was invariably preferred.

England was not exceptional in the desire for a glass production based upon Venetian example and in 1549 eight workmen came from Murano to work in London by order of Edward VI. This was a very short-lived venture and by *c.* 1552 only one remained. A further attempt was made in 1565, under Cornelius De Lannoy, but this too was a failure as De Lannoy was almost certainly an impostor. Protestant immigrants from Lorraine were brought to England in 1567, under privilege from Queen Elizabeth, by Jean Carré, a merchant from Antwerp and Arras. These workmen made window glass and possibly some vessels in the style of the Rhineland and the Netherlands, but they were not concerned in the manufacture of good quality glass derived from Venetian inspiration.

It was not until 1570, with the establishment of the Crutched Friars Glasshouse in London under the direction of Jean Carré, that the production of glass in the Venetian tradition was finally achieved. This was largely due to the work of Jacopo Verzelini, who came from Antwerp to work for Carré in 1571.

Verzelini (1522–1606), a Venetian by birth, ran Crutched Friars after the death of Carré in 1572 and is the most important figure in the history of early glass-making in England. On 15th December 1575, he was granted a patent for the manufacture of glass on the Venetian pattern for twenty-one years, which specifically stated that he was to train English workmen in the craft. The large Venetian import was forbidden and the first important pieces of English glass were made in the Broad Street glasshouse, probably established in the same year. Verzelini was granted papers of denizenship in 1576 and retired from the glasshouse to his estate in Kent in 1592. He died in London on 20th January 1606.

The series of glasses dating from the Verzelini period are few in number and difficult to identify with any certainty, as they are similar to other Venetian-inspired glass of the period. Those with English inscriptions are the only vessels for which a definitive attribution is possible. They are soda glass goblets decorated with diamond point engraving, almost certainly commemorative in origin and usually incorporating a date. Engraved decoration on the Verzelini goblets is ascribed to the hand of Anthony de Lysle, a French engraver resident in London, who had close connections with the Worshipful Company of Pewterers.

When Verzelini retired in 1592, the remaining years of the monopoly passed into the jurisdiction of Jerome Bowes (died 1616). The monopoly granted some right of import and Bowes, a soldier, was concerned with financial gain rather than with the actual glass-making. His monopoly ended in 1604 and for the next few years a series of financiers and speculators, who were not glass-makers but merely interested in exploiting the financial benefits of the industry, assumed control. Patents for glass manufacture were granted to Sir Percival Hart and Edward Forcett in 1608, to Sir William Slingsby in 1610 and to Sir Edward Zouch in 1611.

The most important right of production, however, comparable in effect to that of Verzelini's, was the patent granted to Sir Robert Mansell, amongst others, in 1615. Sir Robert Mansell (1573–1656), a retired Admiral, was in complete control of this particular monopoly by 1618 and by 1623 was the owner of yet another patent. Although the latter granted the right of import, it virtually guaranteed the sole manufacturing rights of English glass to Mansell until his death in 1656.

The substitution of coal for wood, which the glasshouses had been forbidden to use by Royal proclamation since 1615, and upon which all subsequent patents depended, caused some modifications in the methods of glass-making in England at this period. Almost no intact pieces of glass remain from the Mansell monopoly and what there was was probably of a weak metal. In form, the Mansell glass would have resembled that popular in the Venetian-inspired glasshouses of Europe. It is recorded that Mansell employed Italian workmen, including Antonio Miotti between 1618 and 1623, Mantuan Altarists c. 1630, and Paolo Mazzola, between 1640 and 1655.

In 1635, the Glass-Sellers Company, which was concerned originally with the production of serving bottles rather than fine drinking glass, received a royal charter. The Company was later to have a profound influence on the manufacture of English glass after the Restoration of Charles II in 1660.

Following the Restoration, the Duke of Buckingham was granted a patent for the production of glass in England by a Frenchman, John de la Camm. Buckingham not only employed Venetians in his Greenwich glasshouse, but also controlled the 1661 patent for the manufacture of 'crystal glass' held by Martin Clifford and Thomas Powlden, as well as the patent granted to Thomas Tillson in 1663. In 1663, Buckingham himself was granted the sole privilege for mirror glass made by the heavy cylinder process at Vauxhall. John Bellingham, who had worked in Harlem and Amsterdam, managed the Vauxhall works from 1671 until 1674. (The heavy cylinder process was used before the invention of Bernard Perrot for which Louis XIV granted a patent in 1688. A broad cylinder of glass metal was blown, then cooled and split vertically. The split cylinder was put on a bed of sand with the sides uppermost and flattened by exposure to heat).

During this period of general scientific enquiry, the possibilities of glass manufacture aroused considerable interest. The Royal Society was founded in 1662 and in the same year the standard Italian work on glass-making, *L'Arte Vetraria*, first published in Florence in 1612, was translated by Christopher Merret. The Glass-Sellers Company, whose charter was renewed in 1664, actively promoted research into the manufacture of glass and exerted a firm control upon contemporary taste through their enormous import from Venice.

In the historic correspondence of 1667 to 1673 between John Greene, who became Master of the Glass-Sellers Company in 1679, and the Venetian exporter, Alesio Morelli, Greene supplied drawings of his requirements and imported not only large quantities of drinking glasses, but also mirror glass, thus emphasising the still uncertain position of contemporary production in England. The constant demand in the letters for 'bright clear and whit sound metal' is an indication of what was required for the English market.

Unreliable delivery and the uncertain quality of Venetian import caused concern and coincided with the desire for a stronger metal than that of soda glass. The need for a strong metal became more important as the market expanded in the late seventeenth century, and this demand was exploited by the influential Glass-Sellers Company.

In 1673, George Ravenscroft (1618–1681) was engaged by the Company to research for a stronger and more effective metal. Ravenscroft, aided by an Italian glass-maker named da Costa, succeeded and in 1674 was granted a patent by Charles II for the manufacture of 'crystalline glass resembling rock crystal'. He became official glass-maker to the Glass-Sellers Company and was bound to a seven-year agreement to make glass under the Company's mandate at the Savoy Glasshouse and in the experimental glasshouse at Henley-on-Thames, which was run by Hawley Bishopp from 1676.

Ravenscroft's metal contained a high proportion of lead oxide, which had never been used in quantity for the production of glass before. Owing to chemical imbalance caused by an excess of alkali, however, his glass vessels contained incipient decay, which resulted in almost immediate surface deterioration.

'Crizzling', or decay, was obviously of immediate concern and in 1676 an announcement was made to the effect that it had been rectified and that a seal had been placed on the glass to guarantee purity. This statement was repeated three times in advertisements, but the famous seal of the raven's head, derived from the arms of the Ravenscroft family, was not mentioned until 1677. In 1677, the Glass-Sellers Company announced that all glass was now being made with a seal and offered an exchange or refund in the case of 'crizzled' vessels. The Ravenscroft seal, however, had probably been in operation for several months before this official statement was issued.

The sealing of glass vessels was not solely the prerogative of Ravenscroft or of the Glass-Sellers Company. The Ratcliff Factory of John Bowles (1640–1709) in partnership with William Lillington used a seal of a female figure shooting with a bow, and the Falcon works at Southwark, owned by Francis Jackson and John Straw, is recorded as manufacturing sealed work in 1683. The practice of sealing drinking glasses and other domestic vessels did not survive into the eighteenth century, however, and in fact had virtually been discontinued by 1684, except for glass bottles.

Ravenscroft's revolutionary discovery was unique to this country. Oxide of lead had been used before 1674, but only for coloured glass and glazes, and not as an integral part of the mass. The search for a stronger metal encouraged experiment in different constituents. Ground flint was almost certainly tried as an alternative to the addition of imported Venetian pebbles, a vital constituent in the common method of producing soda glass. The proportion of alkali, in the form of potash rather than imported *barilla* or Spanish soda ash, was increased to accelerate the fusion of the ground flint, and it was this excess of alkali that, as has already been mentioned, led to crizzling. To rectify this potentially disastrous decomposition part of the alkali was replaced by oxide of lead to encourage fusion. Gradually, the proportion of oxide of lead was increased, until it made up about thirty per cent of the total mass. Flint was soon abandoned in favour of sand. Metal of this type is occasionally referred to as flint glass, but it is in fact a lead glass, and the combination of oxide of lead and potash is peculiar to the English glass industry of the period.

Lead crystal glass was totally different from anything that had been made in England before. It was heavier and far more lustrous than Venetian *cristallo,* with an oil-like quality of great brilliance. It could not be blown so thinly as soda glass and Ravenscroft's early vessels were heavy northern baroque forms. Their design was usually based upon Continental prototypes, sometimes decorated with thick pincered trailing, an applied decoration referred to as 'nipt diamond waies'. By the end of the seventeenth century, production of lead glass had become the dominant feature of English output. There was a small export trade, mainly to Holland where lead glass was in considerable demand for diamond point engraving. It was Ravenscroft's development of this unique metal that laid the foundations for the widespread manufacture of glass in eighteenth-century England.

By the beginning of the eighteenth century, the reliance on Continental prototypes and such ornament as 'nipt diamond waies' had been abandoned. Glass-makers soon recognised the radically different properties and potential of lead glass and, from the late seventeenth century, trailed and pincered work was abolished in favour of the baluster stem glass, used widely until *c.* 1750.

The baluster stem glass – the classical English drinking vessel – was entirely appropriate in form to the peculiar qualities of the new metal. The solidity and weight of the metal and the beautiful play of light on its surface were very suitable for undecorated simplicity. The lack of ornament in the plain bowls and stems of drinking glasses made in the early eighteenth century are a reflection of the harmony and proportion in form and decoration common to the contemporary decorative arts of the time.

The use of the baluster, which originated in Venice, gave rise to a wide variety of differing shapes, themselves a specialist study. Between the beginning of the century and the end of the reign of Queen Anne in 1714, the undecorated funnel-shaped bowls of the glasses were invariably of a height not less than that of the stem. In the early baluster stems the feet were almost flat and were ringed.

The Treaty of Utrecht in 1713 stimulated German influence in Western Europe and the export of German glass, and following the accession of George I in 1714, there was some reflection of contemporary German taste and the Silesian stem, c. 1714–1715, began to be made in England. This ribbed and shouldered stem, often moulded, probably derived from Hesse and from Western Germany and was used mainly for the stems of sweetmeat glasses. It was rarely made after 1720.

In reflection of contemporary design the glasses made during the reign of George I (1714–1727) were sometimes of a lighter appearance and less massive in form with frequently 'waisted' or curving bowls and with longer stems and, in later versions, with a characteristic 'domed' foot.

The unadorned simplicity of these glasses, often described as 'balustroids' or as 'light balusters' was eventually displaced by glasses of much greater elaboration. The variety and style of these later forms coincided with the Rococo and, from c. 1745, a wider and more decorative range of drinking glasses was in production.

The method of drawing the stem from the bowl was common

throughout the eighteenth century. This simple form, adapted from Venetian or from Netherlandish glass, varied in size according to contemporary fashion; drawn stem glasses were heavier in the baluster period than in the mid-eighteenth century. From this method the air twist stem of the 1750s and 1760s was developed.

The more solid drawn stem glasses frequently had an air bubble in the stem and clusters of air bubbles or beads were occasionally used as decorative ornament in the 1720s and 1730s. It was from the use of an air bubble that the air twist stem glass, which was in fact recorded as early as 1737, was developed.

The introduction of the air twist stem coincided with the desire for lighter and more fanciful rococo objects, and the terms of the Excise Act of 1745 encouraged this practice.

The Act was passed to levy money for the French wars, and the glass industry was taxed heavily on the weight of materials used to produce the glass metal. In consequence, the glass-makers had to produce the maximum number of objects from the minimum amount of material, and were forced to produce glasses whose cost was governed by the amount of decoration rather than by the amount of actual metal in use. The duty levied by weight affected the amount of lead used in manufacture, so that metal produced after 1745 as less oily and more watery in appearance and the heavy ringed font was abandoned.

The air twist stem was produced extensively following the Excise Act. It was made by denting the base of the bowl, already formed and warm. The small holes were then covered with a lump of warm metal and the entrapped air expanded and was elongated as the stem was drawn out.

In the early stems of the 1740s the threads caused by the expanding air were frequently faulty and the stems were occasionally knopped. The wide range of air twist stems produced in the 1750s and 1760s was far more elaborate and of an obvious technical sophistication.

It became common practice to use an opaque white or

coloured thread in a decorative technique similar to the filigree work used in German and Netherlandish glass made in the Venetian pattern. The stems were made by placing rods of white or coloured glass around a cylindrical mould. The rods were then picked up on a lump of molten metal and, after being covered with clear glass, were drawn out into an elaborate and twisted cane. These stems, which were very long compared with the height of the bowl, were not in full production until the late 1750s.

The bowls on air twist stems in the 1740s and very early 1750s were simple drawn funnels. By the middle of the century, however, the ogee and double ogee bowl became popular, in reflection of contemporary decoration. By the 1770s the bowls had become narrow and slender.

Sweetmeat dishes, jelly glasses and some candlesticks had been made before 1750 and so-called Hogarth glasses, which were almost stemless, were manufactured at the same time as the more elegant and sophisticated air twist stem. At this same period, firing glasses were produced, the heavy foot of the firing glass being intended for hammering on the table during a convivial gathering.

Little cut-glass or wheel engraving has survived from before 1750 and it is possible that some very early pieces may have been used for cullet when the Act of 1745 increased the price of raw materials. There is no sign of German-inspired cut-glass in England before the eighteenth century, but from the 1750s cutting, engraving and the manufacture of more decorative glass increased.

As early as 1709, imported German cut-glass was advertised for sale in London and it was probably here that the Silesian stem first appeared. Early cutting and wheel engraving in England was the work of independent glass-cutters, almost certainly of German origin, for whose work English metal was eminently suitable. The first works cutting room, as such, was not established until c. 1750, when Christopher Fitzsimons of the Round Glasshouse in Dublin set one up with some London cutters. This method spread to Stourbridge, c. 1770, and by the 1780s was in common practice. By c. 1790, steam-driven plant was used in Stourbridge, the centre of the English glass industry of the eighteenth century. The use of steam-driven plant was almost universal by c. 1810.

English cutting and engraving was very inferior to contemporary German work, and was little in evidence before the 1740s. The shallow slicing and simple diamond facets of this early period were more like the work of the glass grinders, who not only ground mirror plate but also bevelled and shaped it.

The relatively simple and unsophisticated English wheel engraving was first practised c. 1735–1745. Bordered and scrolled decoration, with formal flowers, wine leaves and grapes, were common until the late 1770s. The engraved ornament was often appropriate to the contents of the glasses, with grapes and vine leaves on wine glasses, hops and barley on ale glasses, and apple-trees on cider glasses. There was some chinoiserie decoration, reflecting the use of chinoiserie in contemporary decorative art, and some armorial engraving closely related to that appearing upon contemporary silver. Commemorative engraving was constantly produced, the most notable groups of commemorative glasses being the 'privateer' glasses made between c. 1756 and 1760, the glasses made in commemoration of the Seven Years' War of 1756–1763, and the Jacobite glasses made in commemoration of the Stuart cause.

Early Jacobite glasses made between 1720 and 1745, with baluster stems or drawn stems and with occasional diamond point engraving, are rare. 'Amen' glasses, bearing part of the Jacobite anthem and the cypher of the Old Pretender (1688–1766), the so-called James VIII, were frequently of this type and have very often been faked.

The majority of Jacobite glasses were made after 1745 and before the death of the Old Pretender in 1766. They were mostly wheel-engraved and it is thought that some of them may have been made in Newcastle and decorated elsewhere.

The most common Jacobite motif was the rose, supposedly

representing the Crown of England. A large number of Jacobite symbols were engraved on contemporary wine glasses, including the very rare portrait of the Old Pretender. The portrait of the Young Pretender (1720–1788), various Jacobite mottoes such as *'Fiat'*, together with symbolic emblems such as bees, butter-flies, sunflowers and roses, are all represented in the wheel engraving used on these glasses.

Decanters, a development of the decanter bottles or serving bottles of the seventeenth century, were in production *c.* 1750, with ground glass stoppers in evidence by the middle of the eighteenth century. Engraved labels were in use as a practical form of decoration *c.* 1775. The club-shaped decanter of the mid-eighteenth century, with a spire-shaped stopper, was replaced by a lighter, mallet-shaped form, *c.* 1760, in which the stopper represented a vertical disc. These lighter decanters were made until the late eighteenth century, when mushroom stoppers and ringed necks became popular until *c.* 1850.

By the 1760s and 1770s, glass was being used for lighting purposes, as in the chandeliers made for the Assembly Rooms in Bath in 1770 and 1771. Glass candlesticks had been made prior to this and glass was put to a wide range of uses during the last three decades of the eighteenth century.

The excise on glass was vastly increased following the Acts of 1777, 1781 and 1787, which gave great impetus to the develop-ment of the glass industry in Ireland, as did the Act of 1780 which granted Ireland freedom of trade. It is very difficult to identify the products of individual factories during this Anglo-Irish period, *c.* 1780 to 1825, except where pieces are marked, an example being an impressed low relief on the base of some jugs, decanters and fingerbowls.

The most famous of these markings is *'Penrose Waterford'*, that of the factory founded, *c.* 1783, by John Hill, a Stourbridge glass-maker who went to Ireland, *c.* 1783, and entered the service of William and George Penrose. In 1786, technical direction of the factory came under the influence of Jonathon Gatchell, who became sole owner in 1810. From his death in

1823 until the end of the Waterford factory in 1851, little work of originality or of importance was produced.

One of the widespread theories concerning glass made in Waterford is that it was all of a distinctive and unusual colour. Waterford was, however, not the only Irish factory of consequence in the period and not all Anglo-Irish vessels are of a peculiar colour. Nevertheless, there is a tendency for glass of this period to contain a dark blue tint in the metal, although this is not invariable and is a common defect in old glass. The blue tint is caused by an excess of black manganese, used to counteract the green stain caused by the presence of iron in the glass-making constituents. The slightest excess of black manganese causes a stain in the metal and this is the reputed Irish or Waterford colour.

Other factories for whose work a definitive attribution is possible used similar impressed low relief as a base mark. Markings for *'Waterloo Company, Cork'*, *'B. Edwards, Belfast'*, *'Cork Glass Company'* and *'C. M. Company'* for Charles Mulvany of Dublin, have all been recorded from the Anglo-Irish period.

The Acts of 1777, 1781 and 1787 and the enforcement of the excise tax made the production of heavy cut-glass in England extremely difficult and, as Ireland was exempt, the Irish glass industry achieved prominence and Irish glass could, if need be, be of a more massive and decorative appearance than similar glass manufactured in England.

Coinciding with the desire for heavy cut-glass and for more classical taste, as represented in the work of Robert Adam (1728–1792), English drinking glasses made between 1775 and the early nineteenth century were shorter in stem than those of the mid-century and, *c.* 1780, an oviform bowl became usual. These bowls, with short drawn stems and often with solid square feet, either cut or moulded, are a reflection of contemporary classical form.

In the baluster period, there had been no general demand for coloured glass, although blue and green glass was in very limited production between 1715 and 1745. Purple glass was rarely used before 1745. The increased use of coloured and decorative glass metal coincided with the rococo period and by 1751 coloured glass was being produced in Stourbridge. In Bristol, Warrington and Sunderland a considerable amount of coloured glass was made in the 1750s and 1760s, but it is virtually impossible to make a definitive attribution for coloured glass of this period. Only one Bristol concern is known to have marked its work in coloured glass, and that is the firm of Isaac Jacobs, for which a mark in gold is recorded *c.* 1795.

In the middle of the eighteenth century, glass vessels resembling porcelain achieved considerable importance. These vessels, common throughout Europe at the time, were exempt from the excise tax laid on the glass industry by the Act of 1745. This practice coincided with the rise of contemporary porcelain factories and moulded, opaque vessels in white metal, containing oxide of tin, were made to imitate porcelain. The metal which has frequently been ascribed to Bristol, was most probably produced in south Staffordshire, although opaque white glass was not unique to this area.

The form and decoration of such vessels derived from porcelain. Garnitures, or sets of vessels, were made in imitation of Oriental prototypes. The decorative ornament and often unfired gilding apparent on opaque white glass of this period was copied from contemporary porcelain and carried out in enamelled work. It was the work of independent decorating workshops, who were further engaged in the gilding of coloured glass. Gilding of this kind was a feature of the London workshop of James Giles, notable for the decoration of Worcester porcelain. William Absalon, in Yarmouth, was a similar decorator in the early nineteenth century.

Independent and individual enamelling of singular beauty was produced by members of the Beilby family at the same time as the more commercial ornament of the decorating workshops. The Beilby family, practising in Newcastle-upon-Tyne, enamelled a series of glass vessels with rococo decoration and marked them with their surname. This series is attributable to the period between 1762 and 1774–1778, the earliest definitive authentication being that of 1763.

The two brothers, William (1740–1819) and Ralph (1743–1817), and their sister Mary (c. 1749–1797), produced a unique and decorative form of enamelled ornament, with particular originality from William and Mary. It is thought that William Beilby acquired his technique in the Birmingham workshop of an enamel box maker. Ralph Beilby, a heraldic engraver, silversmith and jeweller, was the master of Thomas Bewick (1753–1828), the wood engraver. A younger brother, Thomas, may also have been concerned in this work.

Similar enamelled ornament in the rococo style was used by other decorators on drinking glasses of the 1760s. Light and fanciful motifs, derived from contemporary decorative art, were painted in white enamel on the bowls of air twist stem glasses in sympathy with contemporary wheel engraving.

The increasing use of industrial methods and the enormous market created by the Industrial Revolution stimulated production of a far more widespread and decorative output in the nineteenth century than would have been possible in eighteenth-century England. Glass in the late nineteenth century could be manufactured cheaply and in large quantities, and increasing prosperity gave rise to the manufacture of glass of elaborate form and decoration, both for the purpose of display and for domestic use.

However, in the Regency period, c. 1800–1830, a period of great technical skill in which the classical standard of cutting was produced, the long period of excise established in the eighteenth century did not encourage experiment. There were never more than about ten Irish factories producing cut-glass and rarely more than fifty similar concerns in England. Nevertheless, glass of the Regency period was copied extensively in Europe, and the Irish factories established considerable export to America. Massive cut-glass, with the emphasis on heavy decorative cutting, was in manufacture until c. 1825. In 1825, an excise duty was laid on glass made in Ireland. As a result of this and increasing industrial methods, the use of such heavy form and overall, decorative ornament declined.

In the following period, between 1825 and 1830, the emphasis was on verticality. Now flat and vertical cutting were used together with broad flutes. In the 1830s and 1840s, concurrent with the revival of rococo decoration, this well-proportioned ornament was replaced by curving and linear form. The use of arched patterns in the 1840s was reminiscent of the Gothic revival.

It was not, however, until after the Royal Commission on the glass industry of 1833 and the removal of the eighteenth-century excise in 1845 that the English glasshouses were encouraged to expand or to develop more original form and decoration. The removal of the excise stimulated a revival in the practice of deep cutting apparent in the glass displayed at the Great Exhibition of 1851, to which the glass industry made one of the largest contributions.

Despite the stimulus given to the production of cut-glass by the Exhibition, there was an international tendency away from massive cutting in the 1850s, 1860s and 1870s. Contemporary demand for globular form and engraved decoration did not encourage massive cutting. Elaborate cutting was not revived on an important scale until the latter part of the nineteenth century, when cutting of extreme complexity was practised in the 1880s and 1890s, particularly for exhibition work.

Throughout the nineteenth century, wheel engraving was constantly in practice. Commemorative decoration, as in the glasses commemorating the death of Nelson in 1805, was very popular, as the heavy bucket-shaped glasses of the early nineteenth century were eminently suitable for ornament of this kind. The firm of Thomas Wood of Stourbridge made a notable contribution to the Great Exhibition of 1851 in the field of engraved glass, and the desire for elaborate decoration and for museum-inspired revivalism was exploited to a marked degree by the use of derivative and engraved ornament. The demand for decorative vessels of this kind was furthered by the use of

globular and hemispherical forms, inspired by classical prototypes. In the 1860's, Grecian ornament and Renaissance arabesques were common decorations and the fern pattern, in use
in the late nineteenth century, was in evidence from *c.* 1862.
The London Exhibition of 1862 and the Paris Exhibition of
1867 were both important for the display of engraved glass of
superb quality and exhibitions such as these encouraged the
immigration of Continental engravers.

The work of the Bohemian engraver, Frederick E. Kny (died
c. 1900), who was employed by Thomas Webb and Sons (1853–
1924, established at Dennis Park in 1856) and the engraving
of William Fritsche and Joseph Kneller, who was employed by
Stevens and Williams (established in 1846) is representative of
this immigration. In the 1880s and 1890s, deep and polished
engraving was used for cutting on rock crystal, possibly derived
from France. Wheel engraving of this kind was exhibition work
for the luxury market.

Throughout the late nineteenth century, elaboration in both
form and decoration was constantly in demand and a further
manifestation of this ideal was in the creation of cameo glass.
English cameo work, unlike that of Emile Gallé, was classical
in inspiration, except in the use of mass-produced articles decorated with naturalistic ornament by the acid process.

Cameo glass, a revival of the technique employed in the
manufacture of the Portland Vase, was derived from the
museum-inspired revivalism of the period. John Northwood
(1836–1902) was the first and greatest exponent of English
cameo work. He produced several cameo vases in the classical
manner, the earliest being an experimental piece, *c.* 1855, which
was later destroyed. Northwood's copy of the Portland Vase,
1873–6, was an important feature of the display at the Paris
Exhibition of 1878, together with the unfinished 'Pegasus' or
'Dennis Vase', *c.* 1875, which won the Gold Medal. At the
same Exhibition, a similar use of classicism was shown in the
cameo work of the French medallist, Alphonse Eugène Lech-
everel (born 1850), and in the word of Joseph Locke (1846–

1938), both of whom were in the employ of the Richardson firm in Stourbridge.

After the Paris Exhibition of 1878, John Northwood became Art Director, c 1880, to another Stourbridge firm, Stevens and Williams. Under his influence, Stevens and Williams manufactured cameo glass on a commercial scale, many of the pieces being the work of Joshua Hodgetts (1857–1933). Hodgetts was noted for his *intaglio* work and for the practice of stone engraving, c. 1889, using a stone wheel fed with water and worked by a power lathe.

Cameo work similar to that of Northwood was produced in the cameo workshop of Thomas Webb, by Thomas and George Woodall (1849–1926 and 1850–1925), both of whom had been in the employ of John Northwood. Cameo work produced by the Woodalls was marked '*T. & G. Woodall*'. '*T. Woodall*' alone was not often used. '*G. Woodall*' (before 1895) and '*Geo. Woodall*' were used alone, the Woodall signature almost invariably being placed on the overlay and rarely, if ever, appearing on the ground.

Thomas Webb's cameo glass, made from 1884, emphasised the creation of shadow by deep cutting. Quantities of cameo glass were made using the acid process, by which the decorative ornament was painted in acid resistant, with hydrofluoric acid to destroy the overlay, thus enabling the firm to produce a large output on a far more widespread scale than would have been otherwise possible. Anonymous commercial work of this kind was decorated with naturalistic ornament and was marked '*Webb's Gem Cameo*' and from the late 1880's, was occasionally dated.

Cutting in some form or another was the most important decorative element in nineteenth-century glass, whether produced for the luxury trade or for exhibition purposes, but throughout the century, there was a constant search for innovation in both form and decoration. The firm of Apsley Pellatt (*c.* 1790–1878) at the Falcon Glasshouse, Holland Street, Southwark, and from 1878 to 1895 at New Cross, originally produced cut-glass on the Anglo-Irish pattern, but was engaged in constant experiment throughout the period. Apsley Pellatt II (1791–1863) was the first English glass manufacturer to make a serious study of ancient glass and he had a wide knowledge of European production. From *c.* 1819, he made *cristallo ceramie* or cameo incrustation by a version of the method used by Deprez in Paris. This process was patented and was still in operation in 1851, when *cristallo ceramie* was displayed at the Great Exhibition.

The condemnation of cut-glass by Ruskin in *The Stones of Venice* (1851–1853) and the prevailing taste for shape derived from classical form encouraged the development of experimental simplicity and, in particular, the use of undecorated blown vessels. In 1859, the architect Phillip Webb (1831–1915) designed table glass for William Morris based on the form of northern beakers. This was made by James Powell and Son of Whitefriars, a firm established in 1835 and involved in much of the experimental and original work produced in the late nineteenth century, and was the first glass to be associated with the Arts and Crafts movement. A series designed by the architect T. G. Jackson (1835–1924) for Morris was also made by Powell's, who had a great influence on the manufacture of hand-made blown glass in England.

Hand-made blown glass of this kind, a reaction against industrialisation, was made by the firm of James Couper and Sons in Glasgow, between *c.* 1885 and 1904. The firm employed Christopher Dresser (1834–1904), one of the foremost designers of the late nineteenth century. George Walton (1867–1933) was also employed as a designer from 1896 until 1898. The original streaky appearance of Couper's glass, known as *Clutha* glass, from the Gaelic for 'cloudy', was an attempt to produce a hand-made art form in opposition to contemporary industrial manufacture. *Clutha* glass, designed by Dresser, was marked with a flower and the words *'Clutha'* and *'designed by C.D.'*.

Experimental glass like this was generally of limited appeal. The demand for novelty, apparent throughout the Victorian era, stimulated the glass industry to design and produce glass of innumerable patterns, with a strong sense of colour. The Bristol industry, important in the eighteenth century, ceased to be of importance in this period and Birmingham, Stourbridge, Gateshead and Sunderland became the main centres for the manufacture of coloured and decorative glass.

There was considerable manufacture of 'peasant' glass, for country and artisan markets, before the Great Exhibition of 1851, with the Nailsea factory being of great importance. Similar glass was produced in the Midlands, the North, Yorkshire, Newcastle, Sunderland, Warrington and St Helens. Wrockwardine and Alloa were also centres from which the most fantastic and decorative pieces of 'peasant' glass appeared before 1851.

The Nailsea factory, founded by J. R. Lucas, was in operation between 1778 and 1878, producing fanciful objects in bright colours. Dark green metal, splashed and spotted in white and with some use of coloured canes, was made. Lucas was originally a bottle maker and the factory made common domestic vessels and bottle glass, which were lightly taxed before 1845, as well as fancy glass.

From 1810 to 1815, the Nailsea factory was under the management of Robert Lucas Chance (1782–1865). Chance was at the forefront of experiments in colour chemistry and was a friend of Georges Bontemps of Choisy le Roi (1799–1884), who was working in Smethwick with Chance Bros in 1848, and who had been concerned with the production of coloured glass in France.

The expansion of coloured and decorative glass production in England was stimulated by the export of similar vessels from Bohemia. The London showrooms of Bohemian and Austrian firms had considerable influence on English manufacturers and thus encouraged the production of cased, cut and coloured glass. At the Manchester Exhibition of 1845–6, W. H., B. and J. Richardson of Stourbridge, established in 1837, had a prominent display of such vessels which foreshadowed the wide range of coloured glass in evidence at the Great Exhibition of 1851.

The water carafe, registered in 1847, commissioned for Henry Cole's 'Summerley's Art Manufactures' and designed by Richard Redgrave (1804–1888), was a foretaste of the interest in decorated glass which was a feature of glass production of the 1850's. The Birmingham Exhibition of 1849, the patenting of silvered glass in the same year and the Society of Arts Exhibition of Medieval Art in 1850 all provided further impetus for manufacturers.

At the Great Exhibition of 1851, elaborate cut, coloured and cased glass, Venetian glass, pressed glass, and glass shaped like ancient pottery, was displayed. Painted glass versions of Greek vases were shown by the Stourbridge firm of Davis, Greathead and Green, and glass decorated with naturalistic painting or by lithographic transfer printing was in evidence. The firms of Pellatt, Bacchus, Osler, Harris, Rice and Company, and Richardson and Company of Stourbridge, produced elaborate and highly decorative objects. As a result of the Exhibition, museum-inspired revivalism and the increased use of technical processes had a far-reaching effect on the manufacture of glass after 1851.

English glass-makers of the mid-nineteenth century also made paperweights similar to those produced in France. Although they were made in similar shapes and colours, they were never of the same quality, either in form or in decoration, as the French versions. They were made in Stourbridge, at Whitefriars and by Bacchus, who modelled theirs on those by Baccarat.

In the late nineteenth century, Venetian influence on the production of 'fancy' glass and decorative objects in thin and coloured metal became evident. The revival and imitation of Venetian glass in the 1840s, 1850s and 1860s, the Bigaglia Showrooms in London and the Venetian style in production at the Falcon works and by George Bacchus and Son of Birmingham, together with a display of glass by Salviati at the Paris Exhibition of 1867, stimulated this influence, as shown in the frail and fanciful objects with trailed ornament and crimped edges made in the 1880s and 1890s. The use of coloured glass

and of acid to create a satinised finish, as well as Japanese ornament from *c.* 1875–1885, were typical of the eclecticism of the
period, further exploited by the increasing use of press moulding.

Press moulding, which originated in America *c.* 1830, was
first patented in England by Apsley Pellatt, who in 1831 was
granted a patent for some form of moulding machinery. Before
the Great Exhibition English manufacturers produced some
press moulded vessels, including tumblers imitative of contemporary cutting. The Birmingham firm of Rice Harris displayed
glass made by this process at the Great Exhibition and ornament influenced by contemporary cutting was common throughout the 1850's and 1860's. In 1864, a star pattern was registered by the Tutbury Glass Company and, in the same year, a
Greek key pattern was registered by the Manchester firm of
Molineaux, Webb and Company. In 1869, Henry Greener of
Sunderland registered a design using a stippled ground of small
raised dots, a popular decoration and similar to that in use on
the pressed glass made to commemorate the Jubilee of 1887.

Pressed glass was made in the Midlands, Birmingham, Stourbridge, Newcastle and Sunderland, the most important manufacturer being the firm of Sowerby's, of the Ellison works,
Gateshead, founded in 1765 and incorporated in 1881. Con
temporary interest in oriental art, prevalent in England and
in France in the 1870s and 1880s, gave rise to pressed glass of
oriental inspiration which was produced by Sowerby's *c.* 1880.

Heavy and sculptural forms, in coloured and opaque, marbled or 'slag' glass, were used for an infinite variety of decorative
objects 'slag' glass being made with the addition of slag from
local iron foundries. It was known as 'agate' in America and
fanciful pieces, often of solely ornamental use, were made in
large numbers by the manufacturers of pressed glass in the late
nineteenth century.

Designs used in pressed glass were frequently registered and
some firms used trademarks to denote their particular production. Glass from Sowerby's Ellison works at Gateshead was
marked with a peacock's head in relief. The firm of George

Davidson of Gateshead, founded c. 1867, used a demi lion rampant rising from a mural crown. The firm of Henry Greener of Sunderland, founded c. 1890, made further use of a lion mark, the Greener lion being depicted with a weapon.

Registration of a design, as a means of protection against infringement of patent, was common practice in nineteenth-century England. In the series of registry marks to be found between 1842 and 1883, glass was categorised as being Class III. The diamond-shaped lozenge, in use as a registration, depicts the earliest possible date of manufacture, together with the day, the month and the year of registration. The Roman numerals surmounting the lozenge denoted the class in which the particular object was registered. Between 1842 and 1867, the year of registration was depicted at the top of the lozenge and between 1868 and 1883, on the right of it. This system was abolished in 1884 and replaced by a system of official numbering, in which registered glass designs were included. It is therefore rarely possible to give an accurate attribution as to the date of press moulded glass with marks like these, as many of the designs were repeated for some years after registration.

The acid etching process also furthered nineteenth century industrial production on a widespread scale. Acid etching was in use as a cheap form of engraving on glass in the Dudley firm of Thomas Hawkes, from the 1830s to the 1840s, and was carried out by J. and J. Northwood and by Guest Bros of Stourbridge, in the 1860s and 1870s.

By covering a glass vessel with acid resistant, creating the desired pattern and exposing the now patterned vessel to acid, large quantities of cheap, effective and elaborately decorated objects could be manufactured with comparative rapidity for the increasing domestic market of the late nineteenth century.

In 1861, John Northwood invented a template machine, using wax templates, to facilitate acid etching and to increase the production of etched table glass. This was followed in 1865 by another machine for geometrical etching and in 1867, after much experiment, the white acid process was perfected.

The production of glass in England, arising from Venetian influence in sixteenth-century Europe, was furthered by the discovery of lead crystal glass in the seventeenth century. This enabled the English glass industry of the eighteenth century to expand to an unrivalled degree. With the removal of the glass excise in 1845 and the stimulation of the Great Exhibition of 1851, nineteenth-century manufacture was able to develop on a widespread scale, aided by the increasing use of industrial methods.

Further reading

Buckley, *English Glass*, 1925.
Butterworth, *British Table and Ornamental Glass*, 1956.
Honey, *Glass*, 1946.
Thorpe, *English and Irish Glass*, 1935.
Thorpe, *English Glass*, 1949.
Wakefield, *C19 British glass*, 1961.
Warren, *Irish glass*, 1972.

CHAPTER TEN

American glass

The first attempts at glass-making in the American colonies were in Jamestown, Virginia, between 1608 and 1621. Relatively unsuccessful ventures were repeated frequently throughout the seventeenth century and it was not until the eighteenth century that success was finally achieved. The glass-making centres established by Caspar Wistar (1695–1752), Henry William Stiegel (1729–1785) and John Frederick Amelung (died 1798), produced good quality vessels, inspired by contemporary European output, whilst the exploitation of press moulding and the creative genius of Louis Comfort Tiffany (1848–1933) are representative of the technical brilliance and originality of American production of the nineteenth century.

Caspar Wistar, an emigrant from the Palatinate in 1711, established himself as a successful manufacturer of brass buttons in Philadelphia and with the resulting profit established a glasshouse at Allowaystown or Wistarberg in 1739. The Wistarberg factory, some thirty miles south-east of Philadelphia, was set up with the aid of four glass-makers from Rotterdam who were almost certainly of Dutch or German origin. German craftsmen were constantly employed at Wistarberg. The output from the factory was similar to the utilitarian production of contemporary Germany and Holland. Wistarberg was primarily engaged in the manufacture of window glass and of bottles, but some vessels were made from bottle metal. These were German in inspiration and similar to *waldglas,* with *prunts* and with applied ornament, frequently in the form of trailed lily-pads, but were of crude form and poor quality compared with their European counterparts.

On Wistar's death in 1752, his son Richard continued the manufacture at Wistarberg, but probably imported glass from Europe as well. The constant European import did not encourage the American glass industry to develop to any great extent in this period and in 1780 Richard Wistar sold the concern at Wistarberg and production ceased.

It is not possible, however, to make a definitive attribution as to the products of Richard Wistar's glasshouse, although the influence of Wistarberg manufacture established the so-called 'South Jersey' tradition. South Jersey-type glass was soon produced elsewhere and the Wistarberg influence was apparent in similar window glass and bottle houses of New England and in New York State until the mid-nineteenth century.

The first American glass-making centre to make good quality glass successfully on the English and Continental pattern was that of Henry William Stiegel, born in Cologne in 1729. Stiegel, an ironworker, came to America in 1750 and settled in Shaefferstown in Lancaster County, Pennsylvania. In 1758, he took over Elizabeth Forge, the ironworks of his father-in-law, Jacob Huber, and ran this together with Charming Forge. In 1763, as a result of his profitable management of the ironworks and following a visit to Europe, he was able to build a furnace at Elizabeth Forge, where window glass and bottles were made. Stiegel opened a second glasshouse with partners from Philadelphia at Manheim, Pennsylvania, in 1765. Tableware was produced here. A third glasshouse was opened at Manheim in 1768.

The American Flint Glass Manufactory, established by Stiegel, produced glass vessels derived from English and German patterns, which were greatly admired in eighteenth-century America. Colourless, coloured, engraved and enamelled glassware were part of Stiegel's output. The first American cut-glass was produced at Manheim in 1771.

Transparent lead metal, from a formula combining both English and German methods of glass technology, was made at the American Flint Glass Manufactory. It was a potash glass with a lead content and was largely the work of European craftsmen. One hundred and thirty glass-makers from England and Germany were employed at Manheim, including Bristol workmen and German enamellers. Their output was not individual in style but a factory production supplying a large market, particularly the Pennsylvanian German community. Household and drinking vessels were supplied to dealers over a wide area and there was some export to the West Indies. But despite the initial success and large production, the Manheim concerns failed in 1774, and Stiegel became bankrupt.

The sole definitive attribution to manufacture at Manheim is a series of pocket bottles or personal flasks made in the Stiegel factory between 1769 and 1774. These pattern moulded bottles with diamond daisy ornament or with the daisy motif in hexagonal pattern, influenced the production of Stiegel-type pattern moulded objects west of the Alleghenies, 'the Midwest' area centred upon Pittsburgh, in the early nineteenth century.

The wheel-engraved and enamelled ornament produced at Manheim closely resembled Bohemian work, and Stiegel vessels of this type were similar in form and decoration to much European glass of 'peasant' variety. It is even possible that some such vessels were imported European blanks, decorated in America by Stiegel's European craftsmen.

The finest glass of eighteenth-century America was not, however, the Manheim production, but that of John Frederick Amelung, who died in 1798, and whose manufacture was of far greater sophistication that Stiegel's.

Amelung, a glass-maker rather than a promoter as in the case of Wistar and Stiegel, came from Grünenplan in Germany and reached Baltimore, Maryland, in 1784. He arrived in America with the purpose of establishing a lucrative glass-making centre and his venture was well planned and intended to exploit the American market. Aided by the investment of German capital and with letters of recommendation from Benjamin Franklin and from a Baltimore merchant, Benjamin Crockett, he brought essential equipment from Europe together with sixty-eight glass-makers from Bohemia, Thuringia and glass-making concerns in Germany. At Bennet's Creek, near both the Monocacy River and Frederick in Maryland, Amelung established his New Bremen community on a German pattern, in an area probably suggested by Benjamin Crockett. In 1785, the New Bremen Glass Manufactory began production for window glass, clear and green metal. In Amelung's pamphlet of 1787, *Remarks on manufacture,* window, bottle and flint glass are mentioned as being amongst the output.

Very little was known about Amelung's work before 1928. In this year, however, a covered goblet or *pokal* was discovered in Bremen, engraved with the arms of the city and inscriptions 'Old Bremen Success and the New Progress' and 'New Bremen Glassmanufactory – 1788 – North America, State of Maryland'. This vessel, now in the Metropolitan Museum of Art, New York, was almost certainly a presentation piece, sent by Amelung from America to the investors in Bremen. Colourless and engraved vessels of this kind derived from German prototypes, are thought to have been manufactured to promote the New Bremen Glassmanufactory. Between 1928 and 1962 only about twenty-four presentation pieces were recorded, one of which was a gift to George Washington, probably presented with the idea of encouraging interest in an all-American glass industry.

In the excavations at New Bremen carried out by the Corning Museum of Glass and the Smithsonian Institute in 1962–3, there was evidence of a large and highly developed industrial site, but no engraved wares were found. Remains from the manufacture of both clear and coloured metal were discovered, including fragments of blue and amethyst. A quantity of wine glasses imitative of contemporary English patterns appeared, and bottles and flasks in green metal were also found amongst the broken vessels taken from the site. There was considerable evidence of pattern moulding, but there is some doubt as to the constituents of the metal used at New Bremen. The constant experiments in glass manufacture and the production of transparent and clear metal are indicative of some use of lead oxide, although vessels from New Bremen are frequently light in weight and are very like those of contemporary Bohemian output.

In 1790, the glasshouse at New Bremen was burnt out and by 1796 the factory had closed down. The failure of such a well-planned, highly organised and subsidised venture was due partly to over-expansion, resulting in lack of sales. The supposed interest in an American glass industry had not materialised and the lack of trade protection did not enable glass-makers in America to combat the import of European goods successfully.

After the failure of the New Bremen Glassmanufactory, Amelung's workmen migrated elsewhere. In 1799, John Frederick Magnus Amelung set up a glass factory in Baltimore, moving later to the Pittsburgh glassworks established in 1797 by Major Isaac Craig and General James O'Hara. The Galatin Glassworks, founded in 1797 at Geneva, Pennsylvania, was another concern set up with the aid of former New Bremen craftsmen. Glass made in the Mid-West after the westward migration from New Bremen was greatly influenced by Amelung's example.

Other glass factories were established in late eighteenth-century America, although none of them managed to achieve the sophistication of the Wistar, Stiegel and Amelung foundations. In 1769, a glass industry was set up in Kensington, Philadelphia, followed in 1771 by the Philadelphia Glass Works. In 1787, the Boston Crown Manufactory was founded. The production of crown glass began here in 1793, with the help of German craftsmen, and continued until 1827. The crown process, sometimes referred to as the Normandy process, meant that a flat glass for glazing was made by opening a glass bubble and rotating and reheating the metal on the end of a rod until a disc was formed. From this disc, often several feet in diameter, small pieces were then cut for domestic or commercial use.

Glass-making establishments have been recorded in New York City, in Upper New York State, in Germanstown, Massachusetts and in East Hartford, Connecticut. Centres like these were rarely involved in the production of sophisticated glassware, and moulded bottles and pocket flasks with pictorial and commemorative decoration were the most common vessels to be made in late eighteenth- and early nineteenth-century America. The factory of William Pitkin in Manchester, Connecticut, from 1783 to 1830, and the Zanesville, Ohio factory, of 1815, achieved a considerable reputation in the manufacture of glass vessels of this type.

Moulding, a constant practice in American production, was used extensively in the nineteenth century. The demand for European glass, which was not easily met, encouraged the emulation of cutting, thus increasing the development of moulded vessels.

In 1818, the New England Glass Company was founded in East Cambridge, Boston, under the direction of Deming Jarves (1790–1869). This concern, of great importance in the development of nineteenth-century moulding, was in operation until 1888, when the factory was closed after a prolonged strike. The current director, W. L. Libbey, then moved to Toledo, Ohio.

In 1825, Deming Jarvis left the New England Glass Company to found the Boston and Sandwich Glass Company at Sandwich, Cape Cod, a concern of equal importance in the production of nineteenth-century America. This is not to be confused with another Jarves Foundation, the Cape Cod glasswork of 1858. The Boston and Sandwich Glass Company closed after the strike of 1888.

In 1827, Enoch Robinson, a workman at the New England Glass Company, produced a press moulding machine and the technique of press moulding, often used in conjunction with hand-finishing, became general practice in the 1830's. By this method, molten glass was placed in a metal mould in the shape of the finished article. A plunger resembling the interior form was forced into the glass, thus pushing the glass metal throughout the mould and creating an object quickly and easily. This popular method of mass production was taken up by the Boston and Sandwich Glass Company soon after Robinson's discovery, and was used extensively until the late nineteenth century.

American glass-makers were now able to manufacture patterns of far greater complexity than would have been possible by the use of ordinary methods. Although early press-moulded glass was occasionally crude and of relatively poor quality, pieces made in this way were generally very effective. Metal containing barium was often used and gave the glass a silvery appearance.

In 1864, William Leighton of the Hobbs Brockunier factory at Wheeling, West Virginia, a centre for glass-making in America, since c. 1814, developed a lime glass which was of comparable brilliance to, but much cheaper than the lead glass normally used for press moulding. Production of this metal was well established by the late nineteenth century, particularly at the Boston and Sandwich Glass Company in the late 1870s. It was never used at the New England Glass Company.

Press moulded objects, of whatever glass metal, were frequently improved by fire polishing perfected in England c. 1834. This process, in which the finished vessels were reheated in order to obliterate mould or tool marks, resulted in a fine and smooth surface similar to that of cut or blown glass.

The designers of the press moulded glass tended to copy the elaborate cutting styles of the era, but lace-like patterns, far more suitable for such a thick, heavy body, were evolved c. 1830 to 1850. Due to their elaborate surface, such patterns were unsuitable for fire polishing and they were replaced eventually by patterns of a more geometrical nature.

Large quantities of pressed glass in a variety of patterns and comparable to the decorative ornament of the period, were manufactured in many centres. Bowls, dishes, plates and saucers were amongst the objects usually made by this process, and particularly cup-plates. These specifically American glass products were made for holding a cup, whilst tea was being drunk from the saucer. Pressed glass was also used for lighting purposes.

Apart from manufacture at the New England Glass Company and at the Boston and Sandwich Glass Company, pressed glass was made by J. B. Lyon of Pittsburgh from 1849, and by the Curling factory at Fort Pitt, in Pennsylvania, originally founded in 1826. The Jersey Glass company near New York was a similar concern. Many pieces of pressed glass were marked, sometimes with the initials of the maker, *'B and S Glass Company'* together with *'Sandwich'* being possibly of most importance.

English press moulding was greatly influenced by the Americans in the late nineteenth century, and the makers of cut-glass in America were put to severe competition.

Glass-cutting in America followed in the wake of European cutting until the 1830's, when the use of lead glass became widespread. In 1830, the Baldwin Bill established the collection of port dues and formulated high tariffs, which protected American manufacture and helped to exclude foreign import. The result was a boom in the American glass industry which stimulated the production of a national and less derivative style. It was not until *c.* 1865 that serious competition from press moulding became apparent, although a large cut-glass exhibit at the Centennial Exhibition in Philadelphia in 1876 caused both public and commercial interest. The enormous increase in trade and the development of the American railway system encouraged a considerable revival in glass-cutting from the 1880's. The use of gas furnaces, electrically-aided cutting machinery and better raw materials were also contributory factors to this expansion.

Like the glass industries of nineteenth-century Europe, the Americans made fanciful, coloured and decorative objects that were frequently of little or no practical purpose. The contemporary European fashion for museum-inspired revivalism was rarely followed, but paperweights were made on the European pattern in the mid-nineteenth century, as they were elsewhere.

American paperweights were manufactured at the New England Glass Company, under the aegis of François Pierre from Baccarat, at the Boston and Sandwich Glass Company, which employed Nicholas Lutz from Saint Louis, and by the Brooklyn firm of John L. Gilliland.

The rapid and increasing expansion of late nineteenth-century industrial development and the vast wealth of America provided enormous encouragement for the production of art glass between c. 1875 and 1900. The fashion for colourful and ornamental glass vessels of purely decorative value, common throughout Europe from the 1850's, had profound influence on American manufacturers of the day and, throughout this period, American and English development was closely linked both in inspiration and in technology.

The production of art glass in America undoubtedly grew from the observation and adaptation of English prototypes of the mid-nineteenth century. Silvered and opaque glass was developed in the 1850's following English example. The American industry was influenced by the products of the Richardson firm in Stourbridge, which was of very high repute and of great importance in the exploitation of decorative and ornamental glass, and there was some migration of English glassmakers to America during this period.

In c. 1855, William L. Smith and his sons, Alfred and Henry, glass decorators from Stourbridge, emigrated to America and entered the employ of the Boston and Sandwich Glass Company, for whom they worked for some time and for whom they occasionally continued as independent decorators after they had left the firm. In 1871, Alfred and Harry Smith were employed by William Libbey at the Mount Washington Glass Works in New Bedford. In 1874, they leased the decorating shop from Libbey, and by c. 1876 were independently established, working upon blanks supplied by American, German and Bohemian factories. This decorated glass, termed 'ring' or Smith Brothers, was a feature of the output of the Mount Washington Glass Works, but was also produced elsewhere.

Some mould blown vessels with Smith Brothers ornament were marked by a lion rampant within a shield.

Decorated opalines were superseded in the 1880's by a series of shaded and coloured glass vessels, frequently of extraordinary colouring and bizarre appearance.

In 1883 an English craftsman, Joseph Locke (1846–1938), who had emigrated in 1882 but had been employed by Richardsons of Stourbridge, developed *Amberina* while working for the New England Glass Company. This was an immediately popular form of art glass, in which the tonality of the vessel ranged from amber to deep red, the colour ranging from base to rim. *Amberina* was soon being produced on a large scale but was copied by the Mount Washington Glass Company. Mount Washington, under threat of legal action from the New England Glass Company, renamed their version *Rose Amber,* although both *Amberina* and *Rose Amberina* have since been recorded from this particular manufacturer.

In 1885, Frederick S. Shirley of Mount Washington, the 'Headquarters in America for Art Glass Wares', was granted a patent for the highly successful *Burmese Ware. Burmese Ware,* an opaque and shaded glass produced with gold and uranium oxides and with a satinised finish obtained from acid, was manufactured in England at Stourbridge from 1886 by Thomas Webb and Sons, under licence from Mount Washington. English Burmese Ware was marked on the base *'Thos. Webb and Sons, Queen's Burmese Ware, patented'.*

In 1886, Shirley obtained a patent for *Satin Glass,* or *Pearl Satin Ware,* a very popular form of art glass in which the satinised or plush surface was created by dipping the vessel in hydrofluoric acid or by exposing it to acid fumes. *Pearl Satin Ware,* like *Burmese Ware,* was in production at the Webb firm at Stourbridge from 1886.

Yet another form of American art glass was *Plated Amberina,* patented by Edward D. Libbey at the New England Glass Company in the same year. *Plated Amberina* was manufactured in very limited numbers from 1886 and was a pattern moulded cased glass, in which *Amberina* was used as an overlay upon opaque white metal.

Agata Glassware was a rare form of art glass made by the New England Glass Company. This stained and blotched metal, with purple or brown markings, was developed by Joseph Locke in 1887. The glass vessel was covered with stain or mineral colour and was exposed to spotting by alcohol, benzine or naphtha. The mottled or spotted surface was then fired in.

Throughout this period, the Mount Washington Glass Company made a wide range of art glass. Opaque and gilded glass was much in evidence, with *Albertine, Crown Milano* and *Napoli* amongst the most noteworthy designs. *Royal Flourish,* unlike the other patterns, was a transparent and thin metal, with raised gilding and stained ornament.

Acid etched cameo work, as practised at Stourbridge, was made at Mount Washington, although the practice of cameo cutting was not widespread in America. Similar ornament to that used in the contemporary English factories, such as classical ornament on an opaque ground and lightly coloured decoration in pink, blue and yellow, was produced.

During this period, there was a large market for art glass amongst the various plating companies of America, who provided the elaborate metal mounts with which fanciful and highly ornamental pieces of glass were frequently embellished. Mounts such as these, sometimes of silver, although more usually plated, were manufactured in large numbers. A trade outlet for the Mount Washington Glass Company was the Fairpoint Manufacturing Company of New Bedford, Massachusetts, founded in 1880 and a noted manufacturer of such mounts. In 1894, this firm absorbed the Mount Washington factory.

Of all forms of late nineteenth-century art glass produced in America, perhaps one of the most immediately memorable was *Peachblow,* the best of which was made by the Hobbs Brockunier Company of Wheeling, West Virginia. *Peachblow,* a version of the popular tinted and shaded glass of the period, was made under the name of *Coral* at Wheeling, where an overlay of yellow ranging to red was used on an opaque white ground. A further version of *Peachblow,* ranging from white to pink, was made at *Mount Washington* and was copied by the New England Glass company under the name of *Wild Rose.*

The Hobbs Brockunier Company, who formerly made cut-glass and glass with applied or moulded ornament, produced some interesting versions of contemporary art glass. In 1883, William Leighton, Junior, developed a spangled metal in which specks of mica were placed on the gather and then covered with another layer of metal in a different colour. The firm was licensed for the production of *Amberina* in 1886.

Apart from the art glass previously described, decorative glass of America is often connected with the name of Mary Gregory. Mary Gregory, in the late nineteenth century at the Boston and Sandwich Glass Works, was supposedly concerned with the decoration of coloured glass in opaque white enamel, usu-ally with the figures of children and possibly in conscious imi-tation of contemporary cameo work. The majority of these glasses, however, were almost certainly Bohemian, and were not decorated in Cape Cod, but were widely exported from Bo-hemia, and in particular from the Hahn factory, at Galonz or Jablonec, and were possibly copied in America, thus giving rise to the so-called 'Mary Gregory' style.

Art glass of this kind, however, was rarely made for the luxury market, and bore no similarity whatsoever to the superb signed work produced in France at this period. It was the inventive genius and commercial acumen of Louis Comfort Tiffany (1848–1933), exemplifying to perfection the exotic and fanciful ideals of Art Nouveau, which established the import-ance of American art glass on the luxury market of the late nineteenth century.

Tiffany was the son of Charles Louis Tiffany, a noted and highly successful New York jeweller and silversmith. The Tif-fany firm was very fashionable in this era of enormous American prosperity, and had branches in London and Paris and agents throughout Europe. Tiffany's won a prize for silver at the Paris

Exhibition of 1867 and the young Tiffany was, therefore, born into an artistic and cultural milieu, in many respects more European than American.

In 1866, Tiffany began to study landscape painting under the guidance of the American painter George Innes. In 1868, he went to Paris to further his studies with Leon Bailly. Whilst in Paris, he made the acquaintance, through Edward C. Moore, designer since 1851 to the Tiffany firm, of Samuel Bing, a leading Parisian dealer, who supplied Japanese and Oriental works of art to Edmond de Goncourt and other connoisseurs of the day (1838–1905).

Bing, who was certainly in Paris before 1875, supplied both Moore and Tiffany with objets d'art from the Far East and together with Moore had an important influence on the development of Tiffany's taste. Very little is known about him, but as a leading Parisian critic and dealer and later as an agent for Tiffany in Paris, Bing was instrumental in the widespread European popularity of the firm's work. It was through Bing's shop, 'L'Art Nouveau', established in 1895, that the artists, designers and decorators of Art Nouveau found an outlet for their new and often revolutionary ideas in design and in decoration.

During the period 1868–69, Tiffany went to Spain and North Africa. The influence he acquired from Moorish and Islamic art was to be of great importance to him, both as a decorator and as a designer. Throughout the 1870s, he painted, and he exhibited at the Philadelphia Centennial Exhibition of 1876, at which there was a considerable display of Japanese art and of the work of Walter Crane (1845–1915), a formative contributor in the development of Art Nouveau. At the same time he was taking an enlightened and active interest in contemporary design and, encouraged by Edward Moore, he eventually abandoned painting for the decorative arts.

In 1879, in partnership with Samuel Colman and Candace Wheeler, Tiffany founded the Louis C. Tiffany Company, Associated Artists, an American version of the English firm of William Morris and producing embroidery, friezes, panels, tiles and coloured glass, often of marked Islamic inspiration. Associated Artists achieved almost immediate success and rapidly became the leading New York firm for interior decoration. The firm designed the redecorations for the White House in 1882–3, an important feature of which scheme was the glass screen, destroyed by Theodore Roosevelt in 1904. The production of glass was Tiffany's prime consideration during his connection with Associated Artists.

Throughout the 1870s, Tiffany had collected glass and had taken an interest in glass technology, as is reflected in the work of Associated Artists. The stained glass windows of Morris and of Burne Jones and the contemporary experiments of John la Farge (1835–1910) at the Heidt Glasshouse in Brooklyn, were further sources of inspiration, and the use of cullet in the manufacture of decorative window glass, coloured in the mass and leaded, stimulated his later interest in the production of glass vessels.

In 1880, Tiffany established an experimental glasshouse, later burnt out, under the direction of Andrea Boldini, formerly in the employ of Salviati in Murano, and in 1881 he obtained a patent for the manufacture of lustre, inspired by the lustrous glazes of Oriental ceramics and fashionable at this time. Iridiscent metal of this kind had been produced by Lobmeyer in Vienna in 1873, and had been shown by American manufacturers at the Philadelphia Centennial of 1876. It was particularly fashionable in Europe, having been displayed by the French firm of Monot and Stumpf of Pantin at the Paris Exhibition of 1878, where it was described as being 'Chiné Métallique'. The Webb firm of Stourbridge, who had an impressive reputation for fanciful metal, had made iridescent glass from the same year.

Tiffany himself never practised as a glass-maker, but glass manufactured under his aegis was part of an intensely individual production, personally and totally supervised by him. His increasing interest in glass led to the liquidation of Associated Artists.

The Tiffany Glass Company was then set up in 1885, for the sole purpose of manufacturing and developing glass according to Tiffany's ideals. Although this firm was never a financial success, Tiffany carried out innumerable experiments during the 1880s to bring his ideals to fruition. He believed that decoration on glass, in a vessel or in a glass window, should develop from the form and be an integral part of it, rather than created with applied ornament.

The work of Emile Gallé, displayed at the Paris Exhibition of 1889, and the inspiration of Roman glass seen in Paris, furthered even greater experiment in the following decade. By the 1890s, Tiffany had established a wide reputation as a designer and in 1892 his 'Four Seasons', a domestic window made for Walter Jennings, was exhibited in Paris.

In the same year, the Tiffany Glass and Decorating Company was set up, to be followed by the establishment of the Stourbridge Glass Company at Corona, Long Island, of which Tiffany became president. At Corona, Tiffany glass was made under the supervision and direction of an Englishman, Arthur J. Nash (1849–1934), formerly manager of the White House Glass Works in Stourbridge and once an employee of Thomas Webb. In 1884, whilst in the employ of Webb, Nash had taken out a patent for *Vasa Murrhina*, a spangled metal. He was ideally suited to exploit and develop Tiffany's ideas, and a large part of the ultimate success of Tiffany's production was due to his genius.

In 1893, his own house and the Chapel for the Chicago Columbian Exhibition (finished 1893), designed at the instigation of Samuel Bing, furthered Tiffany's reputation as an innovator of outstanding genius. The heavy and flamboyant 'byzantine' style he practised necessitated the use of elaborate and decorative window glass, in which the decoration was integral to the metal rather than painted in. The chapel for the Columbian Exhibition was followed by a High Altar for the Crypt of the Cathedral Church of St John the Divine in New York, and by the execution of a series of coloured glass windows, created for *'La Maison de L'Art Nouveau'* by the Nabis and including designs by Toulouse Lautrec and Vuillard.

In the creation of art glass, Tiffany was concerned primarily with the creation of iridescence, stemming from the patent for lustre obtained in 1881. He regarded his true inspiration, however, as arising from the study of the iridescence caused by decomposition and prevalent in Roman glass. The effect of such decomposition, giving a nacreous and frequently layered vessel, encouraged him to experiment in the use of metallic oxides, regulting in a similar and highly ornamental appearance obtained by the exposure of glass metal to vapour or to gas or by the direct application of a film of metallic oxide on the surface. Tiffany obtained gold lustre using gold chloride, and blue from cobalt or copper oxide. Iron oxide was used for green, manganese for violet and gold or copper for red. Amber was produced from coke, coal or carbonic oxide and black, from manganese, cobalt or iron.

Tiffany's decorative and iridescent wares, of simple or asymmetrical form, and in light or thin metal, were commonly referred to as *Favrile* glass, a word derived from the Old English *'Fabrile'*, meaning hand-made. The word *Favrile* referred to all Tiffany Glassware, not only to the famous iridescent glass, and was a trademark, suggested by Arthur J. Nash and registered with the U.S. Patent Office in 1894. It was stated, however, that *'Favrile'* had been in use since 1892. *'Fabrile'*, the proper spelling, was certainly in use for some early pieces.

The finest period of Tiffany's production was in the 1890s, coinciding with and exemplifying all that was outstanding in Art Nouveau. The rhythmical plant-like forms, the exotic colourings and metallic surfaces were representative of the bizarre distortion of contemporary design and technically, *Favrile* glass was of a superb quality.

The exact chronological order of Tiffany's production is difficult to establish, unlike that of Gallé, as there appears to be no surviving record as to the method of dating at a particular time. Tiffany's firm was involved in commercial manufacture on a widespread scale for the luxury market and it was probably Arthur J. Nash, working at Corona, who evolved the plant-like forms and in particular, the *Peacock Feather* vases.

In the manufacture of such vases, the original glass bubble was repeatedly reheated and charged with small quantities of coloured metal of varying textures. This process was repeated as many as twenty times. Thus the decorative motifs grew with the vessel during manufacture, so that further elaboration on completion was unnecessary – Tiffany's ideal of organic form in glass. Occasional use was made of glass inlay, as in the eyes of the *Peacock Feather* design, but surface application of any kind was normally absent in *Favrile* glass.

As well as plant-like vases, *Peacock Feather* vases and lily pad vases, *Paperweight* vases were being made. *Paperweight* vases, manufactured by a complicated and technically elaborate process, in which floral ornament was placed between two layers of glass metal to give an impression of depth to the design, were an early proof of Tiffany's inventive genius. *Millefiori* was used as in the decoration of paperweights, hence the descriptive name. Fragments of coloured glass were pressed on to a warm blown form. The form and surface application, now one, were then marvered and covered with an outer layer. The whole method of manufacture was an extremely difficult process because of the fragility of the material.

Agate glass, marbled glass, *Lava* glass, a dark blue metal with ornament achieved by the use of gold chloride, and *Cypriote* glass are further examples of Tiffany's manufacture. The large *Cypriote* vases were a late nineteenth-century American version of the sixteenth-century Venetian crackle or ice glass, the warm body being marvered over a bed of small broken pieces, and were predominantly blue or brown in colour.

Like Gallé, Tiffany was also concerned in the production of glass lamps, and his success as a designer and as an innovator of glass coincided with the introduction of electricity on a large scale in America. In 1885 he was working with Thomas Edison on the design of chandeliers for the Lyceum Theatre in New

York and ten years later, in 1895, the Tiffany firm was engaged in the design and manufacture of petroleum lamps. By 1897, bronze bases were being made for the famous series of lamps with leaded glass shades, for which Tiffany applied his principles for window glass to home lighting. Lamps like these were an immensely profitable and commercial venture and rapidly became popular throughout America. The Tiffany firm was concerned in the manufacture of lamps long after the production of art glass ceased.

Following the Paris Exhibition of 1900 and with the waning of Art Nouveau, Tiffany set up yet another firm, Tiffany Studios in 1902, which was engaged in the manufacture and sale of jewellery, ceramics and lamps. The manufacture of glass continued with surprisingly little variation until 1928.

As already mentioned, the exact chronological order of Tiffany's production is almost impossible to establish, because pieces were only marked on leaving stock. Art glass manufactured by Tiffany was marked with a signature, with letters, numbers and with the words 'Tiffany' or 'Favrile', either alone or in combination. 'L.C.T.', 'L.C. Tiffany/Favrile' and 'Louis C. Tiffany/Favrile' were common forms of signature, frequently used together with letters or with numbers. Fine art glass of a less commercial variety bore a complete signature.

Unmarked vessels, unsigned or numbered, were those purchased by employees or those from remaining stock sold in or after 1928 when production ceased.

Pieces marked 'O' are thought to have been special orders, the system recording numbers over 10,000. 'A Coll.' denotes vessels from Tiffany's personal collection, of which there are less than 250 pieces with this particular marking.

A trademark 'T.G.D.Co.', engraved in a circle, was issued in 1894. In many cases this took the form of a paper label rather than an engraving, and it was certainly in use prior to the official date of issue in 1894. Some earlier labels than 1892 were marked with 'Tiffany Fabrile'.

Tiffany's glass was sold through carefully chosen retailers and sales were highly organised on a commercial basis. The glass only appeared on a very limited market, to order, so that prices could be fixed by Tiffany's and were not subjected to fluctuation. If, after three months, a piece remained unsold, it was returned to stock and if still unsold after passing through three different retailers, it was then sold at a fixed price to an employee, given away or broken.

Tiffany's distinctive and individual art glass was never sold on a large scale outside America, although European attempts were made to copy it, in particular at the turn of the century by the Lötz factory at Klostermühle in Austria (founded 1830) and in some of the Bohemian factories. Tiffany himself was never as completely inventive as Gallé and did not exert such a powerful influence on other designers. The manufacture of his art glass coincided with the ornamental and flamboyant period of decorative art of the late nineteenth century and with an era of enormous American wealth, and is symbolic of the luxury and exotic taste of the period. The prime importance of the American glass industry in relation to the general development of European glass was not, however, the influence of Tiffany, but rather the innovation of industrial processes such as press moulding.

Further reading

Amaya, *Tiffany Glass*, 1967.
Daniel, *Cut and Engraved Glass*, New York, 1950.
Garner, 'Tiffany Glass' in *Discovering antiques*, vol. 5, 1971.
Grover, *Art Glass Nouveau*, Vermont, 1967.
Hunter, *Stiegel Glass*, New York, 1950.
Koch, *Louis C. Tiffany's Glass, Bronzes, Lamps*, 1971.
McKearin, *American Glass*, New York, 1941.
Polak, *Modern Glass*, 1962.
Revi, *American art nouveau glass*, New York, 1968.
Revi, *American pressed glass and figure bottles*, New York, 1964.

Revi, *C19 Glass*, New York, 1959.

Watkins, *Cambridge glass*, New York, 1930.

Wilson, 'Early Glass, Wistar and Stiegel' in *Discovering antiques*, vol. 3, 1971.

Wilson, Amelung and the Minor Glassworks in *Discovering antiques*, vol. 4, 1971.

Wilson, 'Art Glass in America in *Discovering antiques*, vol. 5, 1971.

Bibliography

The bibliography provides a wider and more general selection of books as well as including those recommended for further reading at the end of each chapter.

The standard and most important source of information for the general study of glass is :
Honey, *Glass,* H.M.S.O., Victoria and Albert Museum, 1946.

Amaya, *Tiffany glass,* 1967.
Amic, *L'opaline Française au XIXe Siècle,* 1952.
Ash, *Dictionary of British Antique Glass,* Published during 1975. *Nos Jours,* 1955.
Barrelet, *La Verrerie en France,* 1955.
Barret, *Blown and Pressed American Glass,* Bennington Museum, Vermont.
Barret, *Identification of American Art Glass,* Bennington Museum, Vermont.
Barret, *Popular American Ruby Stained Pattern Glass,* Bennington Museum, Vermont.
Beard, *C19 Cameo Glass,* 1956.
Bolitho, *The Glasshouse, Jamestown, Virginia,* 1957.
British Museum, *Masterpieces of Glass,* 1968.
Brooklyn, *Glass and Glazes from Ancient Egypt,* 1948.

Buckley, *English Glass*, 1925.
Buckley, *Frans Greenwood*, 1930.
Buckley, *D. Wolff*, 1935.
Butterworth, *British Table and Ornamental Glass*, 1956.
Chambon, *L'Histoire de la Verrerie en Belgique du lle Siècle à Nos Jours*, 1955.
Charleston, *Dutch Decoration on English Glass*, 1957.
Charleston, *English Glass*, 1968.
Corning Museum, *American Historical Flasks*, by McKearin, 1953.
Corning Museum, *German Glass*, by Saldern, 1965.
Corning Museum, *Glass from the Ancient World*, 1957.
Corning Museum, *Journal of Glass Studies*.
Corning Museum, *The story of American Pressed Glass of the Lacy Period, 1825–1850*, 1954.
Crompton, *English Glass*, 1967.
Daniel, *Cut and Engraved Glass*, 1950.
Davies, *Continental Glass*, 1971.
Dennis, 'Gallé' in *Antiques International*, 1966.
Douglas and Frank, *A History of Glassmaking*, 1972.
Elville, *A Collector's Dictionary of Glass*, 1961.
Elville, *English and Irish Cut Glass*, 1953.
Frothingham, *Spanish Glass*, 1964.
Garner, 'Tiffany Glass' in *Discovering Antiques*, vol. 5 1971.
Grover, *Art Glass Nouveau*, 1967.
Harden, *The Glass of the Greeks and Romans*, 1935.
Hayes, *The Garton Collection of English Table Glass*, 1965.
Haynes, *Glass Through the Ages*, 1948.
Heddle, *A Manual of Etching and Engraving Glass*, 1961.
Hollister, *The Encyclopedia of Glass Paperweights*, 1969.
Honey, *English Glass*, 1946.
Honey, 'Syrian glass' in *Burlington Magazine*, 1927.
Hume, *Glass in Colonial Williamsburg's Archaeological Collections*, 1969.
Hunter, *Stiegel Glass*, 1950.
Kämpfer and Beyer, *Glass*, 1966.

Lee, *Sandwich Glass Handbook,* 1947.

London Museum, *The Garton Collection of English Table Glass* by Hayes, 1965.

Mariacher, *Glass from Antiquity to the Renaissance,* 1970.

Mariacher, *Italian Blown Glass from Ancient Rome to Venice,* 1961.

Mayer, *Islamic Glass Workers and Their Work,* 1954.

McCawley, *Antique Glass Paperweights from France,* 1968.

McKearin, *American Glass,* 1950.

McKearin, *Two Hundred Years of American Blown Glass,* 1950.

Neuberg, *Ancient Glass,* 1962.

Norman, *Engraving and Decorating Glass,* 1972.

Northwood, *John Northwood,* 1958.

O'Looney, *Victorian Glass,* 1972.

Pesatova, *Bohemian Engraved Glass,* 1962.

Polak, *French C19 Glass,* 1961.

Polak, *Modern Glass,* 1962.

Revi, *American Art Nouveau Glass,* 1968.

Revi, *American Pressed Glass and Figure Bottles,* 1964.

Revi, *C19 Glass,* 1959.

Rush, *The Ingenious Beilbys,* 1973.

Saldern, *German Glass,* 1965.

Thorpe, *English and Irish Glass,* 1935.

Thorpe, *English Glass,* 1949.

Thorpe, *The Prelude to European Cut Glass,* 1938.

Toledo, *Early American Pressed Glass,* 1965

Uresova, *Bohemian Glass,* 1965.

Victoria and Albert Museum, *Bohemian Glass,* by Uresova, 1965.

Victoria and Albert Museum, *English Glass,* by Charleston, 1968.

Victoria and Albert Museum, *Glass,* by Honey, 1946.

Victoria and Albert Museum, *Glass Table Ware,* 1962.

Victoria and Albert Museum, *Victorian Glass,* by O'Looney, 1972.

Wakefield, *C19 British Glass,* 1961.

Warren, *Irish Glass,* 1972.

Watkins, *Cambridge Glass,* 1930.

Webber, *Collecting Glass,* 1973.

Weiss, *The Book of Glass,* 1971.

Westropp, *Irish Glass,* 1920.

Wilkinson, O. N., *Old Glass,* 1968.

Wilkinson, R., *The Hallmarks of Antique Glass,* 1965.

Wills, *The Country Life Book of Glass,* 1966.

Wilson, 'Early Glass, Wistar and Stiegel' in *Discovering antiques,* vol. 3, 1971.

Wilson, 'Amelung and the minor glassworks' in *Discovering antiques* vol. 4, 1971.

Wilson, 'Art glass in America' in *Discovering Antiques,* vol. 5, 1971.

Wilson, *Glass in New England,* 1959.

Index